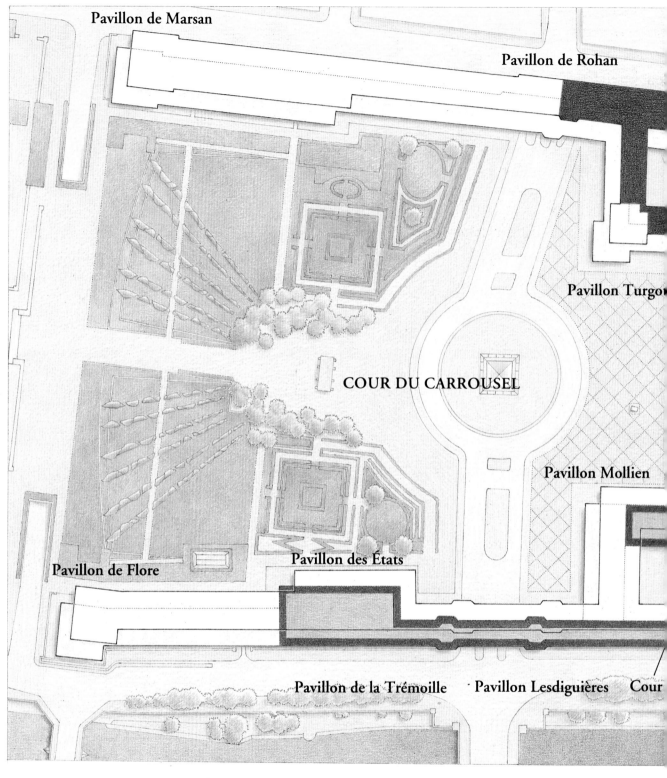

Pavillon de Marsan

Pavillon de Rohan

Pavillon Turgo

Pavillon Mollien

COUR DU CARROUSEL

Pavillon de Flore

Pavillon des États

Pavillon de la Trémoille   Pavillon Lesdiguières   Cour

1ᵉʳ ÉTAGE   Écoles italienne et espagnole

1ᵉʳ ÉTAGE   École française

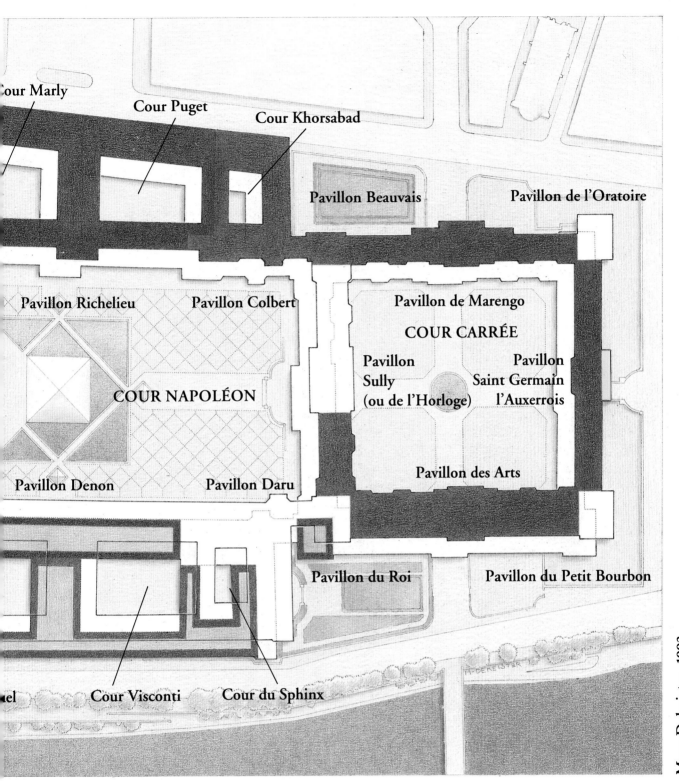

Cour Marly

Cour Puget

Cour Khorsabad

Pavillon Beauvais

Pavillon de l'Oratoire

Pavillon Richelieu

Pavillon Colbert

Pavillon de Marengo

COUR CARRÉE

Pavillon
Sully
(ou de l'Horloge)

Pavillon
Saint Germain
l'Auxerrois

COUR NAPOLÉON

Pavillon Denon

Pavillon Daru

Pavillon des Arts

Pavillon du Roi

Pavillon du Petit Bourbon

Cour Visconti

Cour du Sphinx

2ème ÉTAGE École française

2ème ÉTAGE École du Nord

Marc Dekeister, 1993

THE LOUVRE

Paintings

Michel Laclotte
*Honorary Director of
the Louvre museum*

Jean-Pierre Cuzin
*Head Curator of the Departement
of Paintings*

EDITIONS
SCALA

Réunion des musées nationaux

© 1993, 1995, 2000, Éditions Scala
Passage Lhomme
26, rue de Charonne
75011 Paris

ISBN 2-86656-236-4

Graphic design:
★ Bronx (Paris)

Layout:
Thierry Renard

Photographic credits:
Réunion des Musées Nationaux, Paris,
Agence Giraudon, Paris (pp. 68 bl, 90 t, 177 br), and
Bibliothèque Nationale, Paris (pp. 146-147).

Pages 146-147: *Perspectival view of the Palais du Louvre and the Palais des Tuileries, 1855*. Engraving after the plans by L. Visconti showing the building complex of the Louvre and Tuileries before the fire which destroyed the palace in 1833.

Endpapers: Original plans by Marc Dekeister, 1993.

Contents

Chronology

1180-1223 Philippe Auguste

1190 Under Philippe Auguste the keep and defensive walls of the Louvre are built on a site which is now the south-west corner of the Cour Carrée.

1214 The keep is used to house the royal treasure, archives and furniture store, and also as a prison.

1364-80 Charles V

1365-70 Under Charles V the château is extended to the north and east; the keep is now entirely surrounded by buildings. It is sometimes used as a royal residence but the court is based in the Hôtel Saint Paul to the east of Paris.

1515-47 François I

1527 François I makes the Louvre his official residence; the keep is destroyed.

1546 At the end of his reign François I commissions Pierre Lescot to rebuild the Louvre. The King's collection of paintings is to stay in the Château de Fontainebleau until the middle of the seventeenth century.

1547-59 Henri II

1547-49 Under Henri II the Aile de Lescot is completed (south part of what is now the west wing of the Cour Carrée), decorated by the sculptor Jean Goujon; the Pavillon du Roi is built on the site of the Salle des Sept Cheminées.

1559-60 François II
1560-74 Charles IX

1559-74 Continuation of work on what is now the south of the Cour Carrée.

1564-74 Catherine de Médicis commissions Philibert Delorme to build a château outside the walls of Paris, called the Tuileries.

1566 Construction of the Petite Galerie (now the Galerie d'Apollon).

1574-89 Henri III
1589-1610 Henri IV

1595-1610 Under Henri IV, the Grande Galerie is built, designed by Louis Metezeau and Jacques II Androuet du Cerceau, and the new Château des Tuileries is linked to the Vieux Louvre.

1610-43 Louis XIII

1624-54 Under Louis XIII the Pavillon de l'Horloge is designed by Jacques Lemercier. It is attached to the Aile de Lescot, and to balance this wing another symmetrical one is built to the north.

1641-42 Nicholas Poussin is commissioned to decorate the vaulted ceiling of the Grande Galerie with scenes from the life of Hercules; after initial plans the project is abandoned.

1643-1715 Louis XIV

1659-65 Louis Le Vau builds the north and south wings of the Cour Carrée.

1661-70 Le Vau builds the Galerie d'Apollon after the fire in the Galerie des Rois, on the first floor of the Petite Galerie.

1664-66 Le Vau and François d'Orbay make major changes and enlargements to the Château des Tuileries.

1667-70 The Colonnade, the eastern façade of the Louvre, is designed by Le Vau, d'Orbay and Claude Perrault. The façade by Le Vau to the south is concealed by a new one designed to be in keeping with the Colonnade.

1674 Works on the Louvre abandoned; from 1678 to 1789 the Château de Versailles is to be the residence of the King and Court. Organised almost like a museum, the royal collection of paintings is brought together in the Louvre and the Hôtel de Gramont attached to it. Gradually the pictures are distributed to the various royal residences.

1715-74 Louis XV

From 1725 The official exhibition of the Académie Royale de Peinture et Sculpture takes place in the Salon Carré of the Louvre, from which comes the name 'Salon'. These Salons took place until 1848.

1754 Jacques Ange Gabriel starts transformation of the second floor of the Cour Carrée.

1755 Public exhibition at the Palais du Luxembourg of a selection of paintings from the royal collection.

1755-74 Demolition of the old residence area around the Cour Carrée and Colonnade.

1774-92 Louis XVI

1774 The Comte d'Angiviller becomes Surintendant des Bâtiments du Roi; studies and projects for the creation of a 'Muséum' in the Grande Galerie.

1777 The 'plans and models' of royal châteaux which filled the Grande Galerie are cleared away.

1784 Hubert Robert, Conservateur des collections du Roi, is given responsibility for the organisation of the 'Muséum'. Top lighting installed in the Salon Carrée. The King once again lives in Paris: Louis XVI resides in the Château des Tuileries.

1789 French Revolution

1791-92 After the French Revolution the royal collection becomes the national collection. Seizures of works of art from churches, convents and the nobility. A committee of artists continues the preparations for the opening of the 'Muséum'.

1793 The Museum Central des Arts is opened. A 'special museum for French painting' is instituted in the Château de Versailles.

1796-1807 An enormous influx of works of art into the Louvre, surrendered by or commandeered from Holland, Italy and Germany during the Napoleonic wars.

1800 Napoleon Bonaparte moves into the Château des Tuileries.

1804-15 Napoleon I

1802-15 Vivant Denon Director of the museum which, in 1803, is renamed the Musée Napoléon.

1806 Construction of the Arc de Triomphe du Carrousel, the monumental gateway to the Château des Tuileries designed by Percier and Fontaine.

1810-14 Construction of the north wing of the Louvre along the rue de Rivoli, also designed by Percier and Fontaine.

1815-24 Louis XVIII

1815 After the battle of Waterloo all the works of art that had been surrendered by or commandeered from foreign countries are returned, except about a hundred paintings, mostly Italian, which stay in the Louvre.

1818 The Galerie royale du Luxembourg is created exclusively for the display of work by contemporary artists (subsequently the Musée du Luxembourg).

1824-30 Charles X

1827 The Musée Charles X is created in the southern wing of the Cour Carrée.

1830-48 Louis-Philippe

1838 Inauguration of Louis-Philippe's Musée Espagnol in the eastern wing of the Cour Carrée.

1848-51 Second Republic

1848 The Second Republic decides to complete the Louvre as a 'palace of the people' devoted to the sciences and arts. Restoration and redecoration by Duban; Eugène Delacroix commissioned to execute the ceiling painting for the vault of the Galerie d'Apollon.

1851 Inauguration of the new rooms.

1852-70 Napoleon III

1852 Baron Haussmann orders the demolition of the old residential area between the Château des Tuileries and the Louvre.

1852-57 Construction of the 'new Louvre' by Louis-Tulluis Visconti and later Hector Lefuel; the two palaces are linked together to the north by a series of buildings, thus closing the square with the Arc du Carrousel at the centre. New wings are constructed on either side of the Cour Napoleon producing large courtyards and allowing top lighting to be installed.

1861-70 Reconstruction by Lefuel of the Pavillon de Flore, decorated by Jean-Baptiste Carpeaux, and the western end of the Grande Galerie. The monumental triple arch through the southern wing is constructed.

1870-1940 Third Republic

1871 During the Commune (March-May) the administration of the museum is undertaken by a group of artists, including Gustave Courbet, Honoré Daumier and Félix Bracquemond. The Château des Tuileries is burnt out; the shell is not demolished until 1883 when the view from the Arc du Carrousel to the Arc de Triomphe is revealed.

1895 The Réunion des Musées Nationaux is created with autonomous financial powers respecting purchases. It is run by the Counseil des Musées Nationaux.

1897 Foundation of the Société des Amis du Louvre.

1914-18 First World War

1927 Under the authority of Henri Verne, Directeur des musées, a vast plan to reorganise the collection is begun. The decoration of the Grande Galerie is completed using Hubert Robert's designs.

1939-45 Second World War
1945-58 Fourth Republic

1945 The collection is brought back having been evacuated during the war and the exhibition rooms are gradually reopened.

1953 Installation of Georges Braque's triple composition *The birds* in the ceiling of the Salle Henri II replacing that by Merry-Joseph Blondel (1822).

1958 Fifth Republic

1961 The galleries for nineteenth-century art are opened on the second floor of the Cour Carrée.

1968-72 The Grande Galerie and the Salon Carré are opened and the Galerie Mollien and Galerie Daru restored.

1969 The opening of the galleries in the Aile de Flore and those in the Pavillon de Flore, given back to the museum by the Ministry of Finance.

1989 A first series of galleries on the second floor of the Cour Carrée is opened, devoted to late-seventeenth-century French painting.

1992 Opening of other galleries in the Cour Carrée (east and south wings, and the south part of the west wing) devoted to eighteenth-and nineteenth-century French painting.

1993 The galleries in the Aile Richelieu (the former Ministry of Finance) are opened, devoted to the Northern European schools and to the early French school from the fourteenth to the seventeenth centuries.

1997 Opening of the galleries in the Denon wing devoted to Italian painting from the thirteenth to the seventeenth centuries: Salle des Sept Mètres, Salon Carré, Grande Galerie.

1999 Opening of the Galleries of The Porte des Lions, devoted to seventeenth- and eighteenth-century Italian and Spanish painting.

2000 Opening announced of the Galleries in The Aile Rohan devoted to the Northern European Schools (Holland, Germany, Scandinavia) during the eighteenth and nineteenth centuries.

French painting

Jean-Pierre Cuzin

<
Hubert Robert
Paris, 1733 – Paris, 1808
*View of the Grande Galerie
of the Louvre* (detail)
1796

Canvas
115 x 145 cm
Purchased in 1975

Hubert Robert painted many views, both real and imaginary, of the Grande Galerie of the Louvre. His imaginary views really constitute a set of designs for an ideal museum. When he painted this picture (the finest in the series) in 1796, the Gallery was nothing but an interminably long corridor, lit only by side windows, which linked the Louvre to the Tuileries. The architects who were later responsible for the lighting and redecoration of the Grande Galerie were merely executing the original ideas of Hubert Robert. In this painting several of the masterpieces of the Muséum Central can be recognised, notably Raphael's The Holy Family of François I *and Titian's* Entombment.

Introduction

The French paintings in the Louvre represent well over half the Museum's entire collection; their quality and fame make them by far the most important extant collection of such works. It was therefore decided to divide the Louvre's great paintings into two parts, and that the first of them should be devoted solely to the French School. It should, however, be emphasised that the Museum's other collections, such as the Italian, could well have merited this preeminence, since chronologically the scope of these two parts does not go much beyond the middle of the nineteenth century and, therefore, excludes the Impressionists and Post-Impressionists. The second part, *European Paintings in the Louvre,* covers the Museum's wealth of works from countries other than France and with the first provides for the reader a balanced view of the collection as a whole. In the following pages we shall trace the history of the Louvre itself and of its unique range of French paintings from the beginning of the sixteenth century to the end of the twentieth. Apart from Watteau in the Wallace Collection in London and in Berlin-Charlottenburg, and Bourdon in the Hermitage in St Petersburg, there is scarcely any French artist that can be more fully studied elsewhere than in the Louvre.

We know that François I brought artists from Italy to decorate the Château de Fontainebleau and that he collected Italian paintings. He chose works by Leonardo da Vinci rather than contemporary ones by French artists, such as the Master of Moulins. Probably the only French paintings we would have found in the royal collection would have been family portraits. One still exists and is preserved in the Louvre – the portrait of François I himself, attributed to Jean Clouet, which has now become the symbol of the continuity of the Louvre, a national collection which grew out of the royal collection.

It was not until the reign of Henri IV, after a long period of civil war, that another king was interested in art and commissioned paintings: some of those by Dubreuil which decorated the Château Neuf, Saint-Germain-en-Laye, have survived, but we can really only talk about vestiges of a decorative scheme rather than a collection of paintings. Louis XIII commissioned works from Simon Vouet and asked Nicolas Poussin to decorate the Grande Galerie in the Louvre, as well as commissioning a large altar-piece from him, although Louis XIII was not really a collector.

It was Louis XIV who enthusiastically resumed the traditional role of patron of the arts that had been established by François I. His reign saw the true beginnings of the

Louvre's collection of French paintings, and it was dominated by four contemporary artists, two living in Rome, Poussin and Claude, and the King's two official painters, Le Brun and Mignard. After the death of Cardinal Mazarin in 1661, 546 of the former Prime Minister's most beautiful paintings became part of the King's collection. Of these 77 were French, although unfortunately their titles are not known. Throughout Louis XIV's reign many marvellous works by Poussin and Claude were bought or given to the king. Le Brun, Garde des tableaux du Roi until his death, prepared the first inventory of the royal collection in 1683 and another more systematic one was produced by the miniaturist Bailly in 1710. He catalogued 2,376 paintings of which 898 were copies, anonymous, of dubious attribution, or by Le Brun, Verdier and Mignard. Of the 1,478 paintings which constituted the main collection, the vast majority were French. Many, however, were not easel paintings but decorative works for the royal château. The Cabinet du Roi (the King's art collection) was in the new part of the Louvre created by Le Vau, but these paintings were gradually dispersed to Versailles and other royal residences.

Louis XV, unlike his contemporaries the King of Prussia, the German princes, the Tsarina and the Queen of Sweden, was not a great lover of paintings; in 1770 the fabulous Crozat collection belonging to Baron de Thiers was sold in its entirety to Catherine the Great of Russia. Apart from a few paintings purchased from the Carignan estate, the royal collection was augmented only by canvases or tapestry cartoons commissioned to decorate the royal residences. Nevertheless, this means that the Louvre now owns important paintings by Boucher, Lancret, Vernet, Oudry, Van Loo and Fragonard.

On the other hand, it was during Louis XV's reign that it was decided to show part of the royal collection to artists and the public, a real innovation. From 1750-79, 110 paintings were exhibited in rooms in the Palais du Luxembourg, open at the same time as Rubens'Galerie Médicis, two half-days a week. Among the canvases displayed in this embryo museum, forerunner of the Louvre's, were a variety of French paintings – eleven by Poussin, four each by Claude and Valentin, and one or two each by Vouet, Le Sueur, Le Brun, Rigaud, Antoine and Noël Coypel, Mignard, La Fosse, Santerre, Vivien and Lemoyne.

Louis XVI's reign was decisive for the royal collection and would certainly have seen the opening of the Louvre museum had it not been for the French Revolution. In 1774, the year of the King's accession to the throne, the Comte d'Angiviller became Surintendant des Bâtiments du Roi, an appointement which included control of the royal collection. He realised the role that earlier masterpieces could play in 'reviving' French painting and to this end planned to open a 'Muséum' in the Grande Galerie of the Louvre. He tried to fill the gaps in the collection and systematically ordered works to be reframed in an attempt to unify the paintings. This constituted the birth in France of modern theories of museum conservation and display. French paintings were often purchased: not only history paintings commissioned from contemporaries, but also earlier seventeenth-century works, notably the cycle depicting the life of St Bruno by Le Sueur.

The Muséum Central des Arts finally opened in the summer of 1793, during the Convention. Louis XVI's collection became that of the nation, and the revolutionary leaders, despite enormous immediate difficulties, were sufficiently enthusiastic to bring to fruition an enterprise that had begun under the monarchy. The concept of the museum, which had been growing throughout Europe, now came to fruition. At the

Louvre, however, its realisation took on proportions which no-one could have dreamed of during the Ancien Régime. To the royal collection were added vast numbers of works seized from churches, convents and the nobility, as well as the works which had constituted the collection of the Académie Royale de Peinture et de Sculpture. A museum committee, consisting chiefly of artists, decided which works to keep for the Louvre. When the museum opened the paintings were hung in a very surprising mixture of periods and schools. Among the French paintings were several by Le Sueur and Vernet, examples by Poussin, Vouet, Patel, Champaigne, Valentin, Dughet, Bourdon, Mignard, Jouvenet and Desportes, two by Trémolières, a small Subleyras, a Vignon (now in Grenoble) and even a work by Tournier, then attributed to Manfredi (now in Le Mans). The earliest French painting was *The Last Judgement* by Jean Cousin the Younger, which had come from the convent of the Minimes, Vincennes.

So many works had now been gathered that from 1793 a second museum had to be instigated at the Château de Versailles. This was the Musée Special de l'école Française, where in particular the election pieces of past and present Academicians were featured. The account of 1802 mentions 352 pictures: twenty-three by Poussin, ten by Le Brun and seven by Mignard, also examples by Vouet, Bourdon, the cycle by Le Sueur, Claude, La Fosse, Lagrenée and Vernet. Among the contemporaries were Fragonard, Greuze and Vien. In 1804 this short-lived museum was disbanded.

However, the enormous assemblage of paintings in depots and in the Louvre was only the beginning. The victorious armies of the Republic and then the Empire commandered the most prestigious works of art from royal collections and religious establishments throughout Europe, notably from Italy and, later, Germany. During the Empire Vivant Denon was the organiser and overseer of this unique museum. Thus, for a short time the Museum, which had become the Musée Napoléon, owned a great part of Europe's heritage. It is interesting to note that at this stage the amount of space given to French paintings was small. In the Grande Galerie four bays were devoted to Northern Schools, four to Italian, but only one to the French.

After the Battle of Waterloo the Napoleonic dream evaporated and most of the booty in the museum was returned to its places of origin. Although the Louvre was singularly depleted, this dismantling was not fatal to the collection for, attached to the Civil List, the parliamentary allowance for sovereign's expenditure, it became once again the direct concern of the King. During the reign of Louis XVIII many of the works seized from the nobility and churches were retained by the Louvre, now seen as a great national institution. From this time on the collection turned more towards French painting; from the Palais du Luxembourg, at the same time as the Médicis series by Rubens, came the St Bruno cycle by Le Sueur and several of Vernet's *Ports of France*. Some contemporary canvases were also purchased (David, Girodet, Guérin), and housed in the Musée du Luxembourg, which had been opened in 1818 for the works of living artists.

The most important project during the reign of Louis-Philippe was the formation of the Musée historique de Versailles, and the Louvre was somewhat abandoned. However, after the brief Republic of 1848, when it was again proposed, as it had been during the Revolution, to turn the Louvre into a 'palace of the people' including the museum, the Bibliothèque Nationale and temporary exhibition space, the Second Empire was to see one of the greatest epochs in the history of the museum. With the impetus of the Emperor behind the project, the vast Tuileries/Louvre ensemble was completed in record time, including the gigantic painting galleries (Salle Mollien, Salle Daru and Salle des États) which were such a novely. Of the highly valuable acquisitions made during this period, the Denor La Caze collection in 1869 was the most important. Comprising some eight hundred paintings, it was the finest collection ever bequeathed to the Louvre. La Caze's contribution was inestimable in the field of French seventeenth- and eighteenth-century painting; one cannot imagine how, without him, the work of Largillière, Watteau, Chardin or Fragonard would have been represented today.

With the declaration of the Republic the Louvre became France's national museum and has remained so ever since; gone was the ambiguity of a museum funded by the Civil List of a sovereign. From that time on the purchase of paintings was gradual and methodical, acquisitions being made as knowledge of French painting was extended by art historical research. The generosity of collectors continued; gifts and bequests increased. It was, for example, collectors such as Thomy Thiéry (1902), Moreau-Nélaton (1906), Chauchard (1910) and Camondo (1911), whose gifts of whole rooms of paintings (often filling gaps left by official purchases) to a large extent formed the unrivalled collection of nineteenth-century art now owned by the Louvre. Also important are the collectors' contributions to early French painting such as those of: Schlichting (1914), Robert (1926), Croy (1930), Jamot (1941), Beistegui (1942), Gourgaud (1965), Lyon (1961) and Schlageter and Kaufman (1984).

Above all, the magnificent support of the Société des Amis du Louvre, founded in 1897, has led to the acquisition of some of the greatest masterpieces of French painting, from the *Pietà d'Avignon* (1905) to La Tour's *St Sebastian* (1979). The recent law allowing the donation of works of art in lieu of death duties has meant that major works by Champaigne, Fragonard, Greuze, Prud'hon and Courbet have been preserved for the nation.

The appearance of the rooms devoted to French paintings changed considerably in Spring 1989 with the opening of the new rooms on the second floor of the Cour Carrée. Our collections from the fourteenth century to the end of the seventeenth century are now more amply displayed with many works brought out from the reserve collections. The large-scale works of the seventeenth century, in particular, by Le Sueur, Philippe de Champaigne, Le Brun and Jouvenet, have at last been given the place they deserve. December 1992 saw the opening of the rooms in the East and South wings, designed by Italo Rota and devoted to the eighteenth and nineteenth centuries. The visitor can now walk right round the Cour Carrée taking in the whole history of French painting. The large-scale works of the nineteenth century remain in the admirable Daru, Denon and Mollien rooms situated on the first floor. The Grand Louvre project has extended this programme by permitting access to the French paintings by I.M. Pei's monumental mechanical staircase in the Richelieu wing, to the east of the Pavillon Richelieu. The opening of new rooms in November 1993 has allowed us to rehang the Primitives and works of the sixteenth century, adding considerably to the space devoted to the seventeenth century.

These changes have significantly altered the whole perception of French painting, and enable a more complete exhibition of our treasures and presentation of the great showpieces. The significance of this lies in the fact that our concept of French painting depends so much on what is seen at the Louvre. That image today represents the most diverse aspects of French art and, although it may not be the definitive representation, it is more accurate and complete than in any other museum.

The primitives and the sixteenth century

The Great Exhibition of 1904, devoted entirely to French pre-Renaissance painting, demonstrated for the first time the importance and originality of French painting before the sixteenth century.

The study of fourteenth – and fifteenth – century Italian, Flemish and German painters has come well before that of their French contemporaries, and French works were therefore often attributed to other schools. In fact the concept of 'French primitives' scarcely existed before the twentieth century. Works by Van Eyck and Fra Angelico were exhibited in the Musée Napoléon but not those by Fouquet or Quarton, and the formation of the Louvre collection reflects the fact that in the history of taste French medieval art is very much a new arrival.

However, we should note a few paintings of prime importance that came into the national collection during the reign of Louis-Philippe. These paintings for the Château de Versailles, where the King was forming the Musée historique dedicated to 'all the glories of France', were purchased as historical documents: portraits of *Charles VII* and *Guillaume Jouvenel des Ursins* by Fouquet and of *Pierre de Bourbon* by Jean Hey. Only the sitters were considered interesting and, *Charles VII* was even bought as a 'Greek work', implying that it was Byzantine! These pictures were only later transferred to the Louvre as works of art in their own right.

In the second half of the nineteenth century, just as the history of these works was beginning to be written, succeeding keepers of the collection bought new works and collectors gave others which are still among the most important in the Louvre. *The Narbonne altar-frontal* was purchased in 1852, in 1863 Frédéric Reiset gave *The St Denis altar-piece* by Bellechose and Malouel's *Pieta* was bought the next year.

But it was the year 1904 which saw the real awakening of interest in French medieval art. The Louvre acquired *The Boulbon altar-piece, The Paris Parlement altar-piece* and Jean Hey's *A donor and St Mary Magdalen.* The next year the great masterpiece *The Villeneuve-les-Avignon Pietà* was presented by the Société des Amis du Louvre. After that only occasional acquisitions were made, and the portrait of *Jean le Bon* was offered on extended loan from the Bibliothèque Nationale in 1925. Two extremely rare little paintings, a *Virgin* by a Burgundian master and *Charles-Orlant* by Jean Hey, were part of the collection given by Carlos de Beistegui in 1942.

It is important to stress the extreme rarity of French primitives. This was not only due to their fanatical destruction during the Revolution, but also to the very late appreciation of these works by historians. Only the Louvre can show such a

<
Jean Hey,
called **the Master of Moulins**
Active in central France between 1480 and 1500
A donor and St Mary Magdalen
Circa 1490

Wood
56 x 40 cm
Purchased in 1904

comprehensive collection. This has been further enriched by recent acquisitions, such as the *Crucifixion with a Carthusian monk* by Jean de Beaumetz and the *Presentation of the Virgin in the temple* by Josse Lieferinxe, an artist previously represented only by a secondary piece. Most recently, new works by Nicolas Dipre and Lieferinxe and a precious fragment attributed to Barthelemey d'Eyck, *Christ on the Cross,* have been added to this matchless collection.

The collection of French sixteenth-century painting is also comparatively recent. The glorious exception is the portrait of *François I* attributed to Jean Clouet which has been part of the national collection ever since it was painted for its royal sitter in about 1530. The royal collection must have comprised many portraits: the inventory drawn up by Bailly in 1710 mentions '251 small portraits of the families of past kings and nobility'. All that is left in the Louvre is a small full-length depiction of Henri II, a studio copy of the painting in the Uffizi, Florence. Of great importance to the Louvre is the enormous collection of works of historical interest, mostly prints and drawings, bequeathed by Roger de Gaignières. On his death in 1716 the collection entered the Cabinet du Roi, precursor of the Bibliothèque Nationale. Gaignières seems to have had a particular preference for small sixteenth-century portraits and many now in the Louvre came originally from his collection. Some, which during the Revolution had passed into Alexandre Lenoir's Musée des Monuments Français, entered the Louvre in 1817; others were acquired later. In 1908 the Société des Amis du Louvre donated the highly important portrait of *Pierre Quthe* by François Clouet. Of the more recent acquisitions that of Corneille de Lyon's *Pierre Aymeric* in 1976 is particularly significant as one of his few documented works. Also of note is the purchase in 1967 of the rare *Portrait of a couple.* Thus the Louvre is able to exhibit a comprehensive collection of sixteenth-century portraits. Their precision and concern for the character of the sitter are derived from northern models, features which were to be the hallmarks of French portraiture, and continually developed in later centuries.

Taste for Mannerist art is more recent even than that for early portraits. The Italian artists who came to France in the sixteenth century gave rise to a complete change in taste, giving François I's court a style of painting that was elegant and decorative, very often with mythological settings. This charming Fontainebleau School, with its accent on the artificial, has only been studied during the past few decades and has only recently been represented in the Louvre. The famous *Diana, goddess of the hunt* was acquired for Fontainebleau during Louis-Philippe's reign because it was thought to be a portrait of Diane de Poitiers, Henri II's favourite. Apart from a few other exceptions – Gourmont's *Adoration of the sheperds,* the works by Dubreuil from the chapel of the Château d'Écouen and *The Last Judgement* by Cousin the Younger seized from the convent of the Minimes, Vincennes – the collection has been built up over the past sixty years. *Eva Prima Pandora* by Cousin the Elder was presented in 1922, the very popular *Gabrielle d'Estrées and one of her sisters* was purchased in 1937 and *Augustus and the Sybil* by Caron presented in 1958. Recently a great effort has been made to form a collection which will show all aspects of the Fontainebleau School, with purchases including the mid-sixteenth-century *Charity,* in 1970, and in 1973 *The justice of Othon* attributed to Luca Penni.

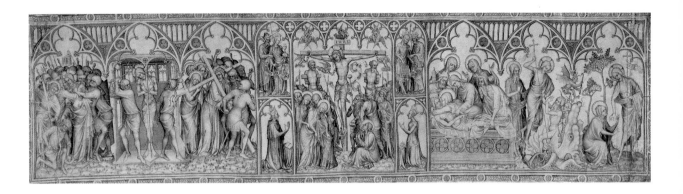

^
School of Paris
Second half of the 14th century
The Narbonne altar-frontal
Circa 1375

Black ink on silk
77.5 x 286 cm
Purchased in 1852

>
School of Paris
Second half of the 14th century
Jean II le Bon, King of France
Circa 1360

Wood
59.8 x 44.6 cm
*Extended loan from the Bibliothèque
Nationale, 1925*

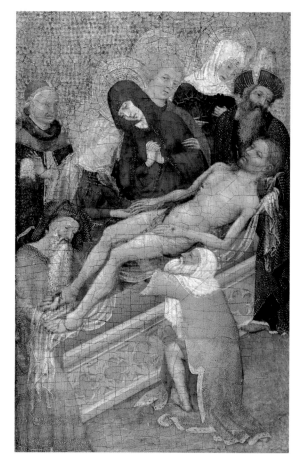

<
**Jean Malouel
Niemegen**
Before 1370 – Dijon, 1415
Pietà known as
'La grande Pietà ronde'
Circa 1400

Wood
Diameter 64.5 cm
Purchased in 1864

∨
**School of Paris
or Burgundy**
Early 15th century
The Entombment of Christ
Circa 1400

Wood
32.8 x 21.3 cm
Purchased in 1869

∧
Jean de Beaumetz
Artois, first known in 1361 –
Dijon, 1396
*Crucifixion with a
Carthustan monk*
Between 1389 and 1395

Wood
60 x 48.5 cm
Purchased in 1967

Jean de Beaumetz, Jean Malouel and Henri Bellechose, working in Dijon, were successively the official artists of the Dukes of Burgundy, Philippe le Hardi and Jean sans Peur. The Louvre is extremely fortunate in possessing a painting by each of them. Characteristic of their work is the combination of refined draughtsmanship with fresh, brilliant colours heightened by gilding, in an attempt to express deep emotion.

∧
Henri Bellechose
Brabant, known in Dijon
from 1415 – Dijon, 1440/44
The St Denis altar-piece
Finished in 1416

Wood transferred to canvas
162 x 211 cm
Presented by Frédéric Reiset, 1863

LE TRESVICTORIEVX ROY DE FRANCE

CHARLES · SEPTIESME · DE CE NOM

<

Jean Fouquet
Tours, circa 1420 –
Tours, 1477/81
Charles VII, King of France
Circa 1445 (?)

Wood
85.7 x 70.6 cm
Purchased in 1838

>

Flemish artist in Paris
Mid-15th century
The Paris Parlement altar-piece
Probably commissioned in 1452

Wood
226.5 x 270 cm
Seized during the French Revolution

∧
Jean Fouquet
Tours, circa 1420 –
Tours, 1477/81
Guillaume Jouvenel des Ursins,
Chancellor of France
Circa 1460

Wood
93 x 73.2 cm
Purchased in 1835

∧
Jean Hey, *called* **the**
Master of Moulins
Active in central France
between 1480 and 1500
Charles-Orlant,
Dauphin of France
1494

Wood
28.5 x 23.5
Presented by
Carlos de Beistegui, 1942

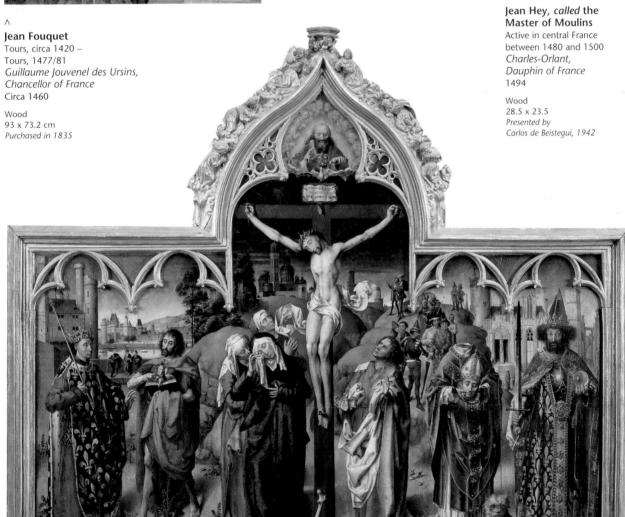

<
Provençal artist
Mid-15th century
The Boulbon altar-piece
Circa 1460

Wood transferred to canvas
172 x 227.8 cm
*Presented by the Committee
for the exhibition of French
primitive art, 1904*

v
Enguerrand Quarton
Active in Provence
between 1444 and 1466
*The Villeneuve-les-Avignon
Pietà*
Circa 1455 (?)

Wood
163 x 218.5 cm
*Presented by the Société
des Amis du Louvre, 1905*

<
**Josse Lieferinxe,
the Master of
St Sebastien**
Hainaut, active
in Provence from 1493 –
Provence, 1505/8
The Crucifixion
Circa 1500/05 (?)

Wood
170 x 126 cm
Purchased in 1962

∨
Nicolas Dipre
Active in Avignon
from 1495 –
Avignon, 1532
*The Presentation
of the Virgin*
Circa 1500

Wood
31.7 x 50 cm
*Presented by Pierre Landry,
1972*

< ∨
Nicolas Dipre
Known at Avignon
from 1495 – Avignon, 1532
The Birth of the Virgin
Circa 1500

Wood
29 x 50 cm
*Presented by the Amis du Louvre,
1986*

>
**Attributed to
Jean Clouet**
?, 1485/90 – ?, 1540/41
François I, King of France
Circa 1530 (?)

Wood
96 x 74 cm
Collection of François I

v
Jean Cousin the Elder
Sens, circa 1490 –
Paris, circa 1560
Eva Prima Pandora
Circa 1550 (?)

Wood
97.5 x 150 cm
*Presented by the Société
des Amis du Louvre, 1922*

<
School of Fontainebleau
Mid-16th century
Charity
Circa 1560 (?)

Canvas
147 x 96.5 cm
Purchased in 1970

>
School of Fontainebleau
Mid-16th century
Diana, goddess of the hunt
Circa 1550

Canvas
191 x 132 cm
Purchased in 1840

∧
Jean de Gourmont
Carquebut, circa 1483 –
?, after 1551
*The Adoration of the
shepherds*
Circa 1525 (?)

Wood
93.5 x 115.5 cm
*From the chapel of
the Château d'Écouen*

>
François Clouet
? – Paris, 1572
Pierre Quthe, apothecary
1562

Wood
91 x 70 cm
*Presented by the Société
des Amis du Louvre, 1908*

*The setting of dreamlike architecture in this picture, clearly
inspired by Roman antiquity, although it is difficult to tell
whether it is under construction or in ruins, is given far more
prominence than the religious subject-matter. Gourmont,
who worked first in Paris and then in Lyons, also executed
engravings in which he often exploited his virtuoso study of
perspective.*

> **Corneille de Lyon**
The Hague, circa 1500 –
Lyons (?), circa 1575
Jean de Bourbon-Vendôme
Circa 1550 (?)

Wood
19 x 15.5 cm
Purchased in 1883

∧
François Clouet
? – Paris, 1572
Elisabeth of Austria,
Queen of France
1571 (?)

Wood
36 x 26 cm
Collection of Louis XV
Entered the Louvre in 1817

> **French artist**
Second half of the 16th century
Portrait of a flautist with one eye
1566

Wood
62 x 50 cm
Presented by Percy Moore Turner, 1948

> **Corneille de Lyon**
The Hague, circa 1500 –
Lyons (?), circa 1575
Pierre Aymeric
1534

Wood
16.5 x 14.2 cm
Purchased in 1976

^
Antoine Caron
Beauvais, 1521 – Paris, 1599
Augustus and the Sybil
Circa 1575/80

Canvas
125 x 170 cm
Presented by Gustave Lebel, 1938

Caron, who was Catherine de Médicis official artist and whose paintings often seem to echo the royal fêtes, shows here the Emperor Augustus on his knees in front of the Sybil, who gestures towards the Virgin and Child in the heavens. The architectural setting, reminiscent of theatre decor, shows the Seine and possibly certain monuments of Paris modified by the artist's imagination on the right-hand side.

∧
French artist
Early 17th century
Portrait of a couple
Circa 1610 (?)

Wood
73 x 96 cm
Purchased in 1967

>
Toussaint Dubreuil
Paris, circa 1561 – Paris, 1602
Hyante and Climène
offering a sacrifice to Venus
Circa 1600

Canvas
190 x 140 cm
From the Château Neuf,
Saint-Germain-en-Laye

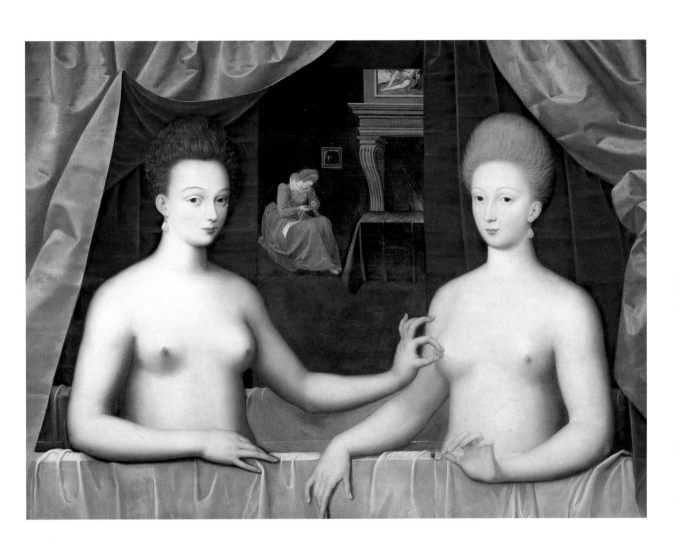

The wide-spread fame of this double portrait rests on its incongruous subject-matter. It was in fact inspired by a famous and immensely influential portrait showing Diane de Poitiers, mistress of Henri II, bathing, which now hangs in the National Gallery in Washington.

∧
School of Fontainebleau
Late 16th century
*Gabrielle d'Estrées
and one of her sisters*
Circa 1595 (?)

Wood
96 x 125 cm
Purchased in 1937

The seventeenth century

The seventeenth century collections of the Louvre
were begun by the contemporary kings of France,
with many subsequent additions which reflected changes
in taste down the centuries.

The collection, formed gradually by different contributions, first reflects the predilections of kings and then those of art historians. Louis XIII acquired few works and the ones he owned came from vast pictorial schemes: the three allegorical figures by Vouet, formerly part of the decoration of the Château Neuf, Saint-Germain-en-Laye, and two large works by Poussin from his Parisian period, *The institution of the Eucharist* commissioned in 1640 and also from Saint-Germain, and the ceiling painting *Truth carried off by Time* bequeathed by Cardinal Richelieu to the king with the Palais Cardinal, now the Palais Royal.

It was Louis XIV who, with unprecedented largesse, formed a magnificent collection of French art, a group of paintings which was essentially 'classical' in taste; a taste which could even be called 'Roman' – powerful and masculine, contrasting and often epic. In fact the collection chiefly consisted of works by three artists who were Roman by adoption, Poussin, Claude and Valentin, the only paintings considered worthy of being hung next to Italian sixteenth– and seventeenth-century masters, and of course it included paintings by the King's official artists, Le Brun and later Mignard. Thirty-one of the thirty-eight Poussins in the Louvre, a collection unrivalled anywhere in the world, belonged to Louis XIV. In 1665 he bought the Duc de Richelieu's thirteen famous canvases, amongst them *The four seasons, Diogenes, Eliezer and Rebecca, The plague at Ashdod* and *The rescue of Pyrrhus.* Seven others were acquired in 1685, and in 1693 Le Nôtre gave the King *The adulterous woman, St John baptising the people* and *The rescue of the infant Moses by Pharaoh's daughter.* Of the Louvre's works by Claude, ten came from Louis XIV, some were bought from the Duc de Richelieu, while others were given by Le Nôtre. Nearly all the Le Bruns, except those seized from churches during the French Revolution, and nearly all the Mignards also came to the Louvre from the King's collection. However, the collection was not confined only to these artists; works by a variety of other artists also feature in the 1710 inventory, among them *Charity* by Blanchard, *Acis and Galatea* by Perrier *Augustus at Alexander's tomb* by Bourdon, and three by Stella, including *The Virgin and St Anne* (now in Rouen) and *Minerva and the Muses.*

<
Georges de La Tour
Vic-sur-Seille,1593 –
Lunéville, 1652
*Christ with
St Joseph in the
carpenter's shop*
Circa 1640(?)

Canvas
137 x 102 cm
*Presented by
Percy Moore
Turner, 1948*

Louis XV bought paintings that showed him to be heir to his great-grandfather's taste for solemn and heroic works. He bought Poussin's enormous *St Francis Xavier* at the Jesuits' sale when their order was suppressed in 1763. At the same time Jean de Jullienne bought Vouet's *The Presentation in the Temple* which he gave to the Académie and which later entered the Louvre with the Académie's collection. The King also bought two fine Valentins from the estate of the Prince de Carignan in 1742.

Louis XVI, however, appreciated another aspect of seventeenth-century art, one that had previously been ignored by royal collectors. Contrary to the 'Roman' taste of Louis XIV, he and his Surintendant des Bâtiments, the Comte d'Angiviller, had what one might call 'Parisian' taste. Poussin was still appreciated, but as the King already had his ancestor's collection he concentrated on acquiring these more 'Parisian' works which were restrained, delicate and refined, with a predominance of clear, soft colours, not unlike the first works by eighteenth-century neo-classical artists such as Lagrenée. An artist who now became very popular was Eustache Le Sueur. In 1776 two large cycles by him entered the royal collection: twenty-two paintings depicting the life of St Bruno painted for Chartreuse in Paris were given to the King by the monks at the instigation of the Comte d'Angiviller; whilst the decorative series from the Hôtel Lambert on the Île Saint-Louis, one from the Chambre des Muses and the other from the Cabinet de l'Amour were also acquired at this time. Louis XVI also bought Le Sueur's fine group portrait known as *A gathering of friends* and *Laban searching Jacob's baggage for the stolen idols* by La Hyre.

Many paintings of similar 'Parisian' taste entered the collection during the French Revolution. Several were seized from the nobility: two small canvases by La Hyre from the Comte d'Angiviller, from the Duc de Penthièvre and the Duc d'Orléans two distinct and elegant Bourdons, and from the Quentin-Crawford collection two rare works by Stella. Also during the Revolution, Poussin's *Camillus and the schoolmaster of Falerii* was seized with the rest of the collection from the Galerie Dorée in the Duc de Penthièvre's Hôtel de Toulouse, and two little works by Claude were taken from the Duc de Brissac. Seizures from convents and churches constituted a major contribution: an enormous number of paintings, often of vast proportions, were thus added to the national collection, including nearly all the works by Philippe de Champaigne now in the Louvre and many masterpieces by Le Sueur, Bourdon, Le Brun and La Hyre. Despite this great influx of riches, paintings continued to be purchased, the government of the Directory buying Poussin's *Self-portrait* in 1797.

Very few contributions were made during the first half of the nineteenth century. However, Champaigne's masterpiece, *Portrait of a man* was purchased by Vivant Denon, Director of the Museum, in 1806 and another portrait by Champaigne was bought in 1835, a double portrait reputedly of Mansart and Perrault. *Apollo and Daphne,* Poussin's last painting, left unfinished at his death, was bought during the Second Empire; but it was not until 1911 that *The inspiration of the poet* entered the Louvre.

With the progressive rediscovery of a seventeenth century which could be termed 'realist' during the last half of the nineteenth century and the beginning of the twentieth, a new visual awareness reinstated 'painters of reality'. The seventeenth-century art of the La Caze collection was realist: besides the two large state portraits by Champaigne and a 'bambochade' by Boudron, there was above all *The peasant's meal* by Le Nain. Between 1869 and 1915 seven paintings by the Le Nain brothers entered the Louvre, including *The haywain* and *The peasant family.* It was during these same years that mid-nineteenth-century artists such as Courbet, Millet and Rousseau, expounders of another kind of realism, began at last to appear in the Louvre's collection. Twentieth-century keepers, who have continued to augment the series by the Le Nain brothers, added still lifes, absent until then, such as those by Baugin and Dupuis, and formed the finest collection of paintings by Georges de La Tour in existence, notably the famous *Christ with St Joseph.*

Recently the Louvre has been enriched by the addition of two famous works by La Tour, *The cheat* from the Landry collection and *Saint Sebastian tended by Irene,* presented by the Société des Amis du Louvre, as well as two masterpieces by the Le Nain brothers, the delightful *Victory* and *The group of smokers* traditionally known as *The guard-room.* The moving portrait of *Arnauld d'Andilly* as an old man by the aging Philippe de Champaigne entered the collection in 1979 in lieu of death duties, and in 1980 the Société des Amis du Louvre presented Sebastien Bourdon's lyrical *Scene from Roman history,* filling a gap in the collection.

Paintings by La Hyre and Patel have been given in lieu of death duties and Le Sueur's sketches for the celling of the Cabinet d'Amour in the Hôtel Lambert were purchased in 1988, followed by a mythological painting by Pierre Mignard in 1989. The most spectacular acquisition of recent years was in 1988, when *Saint Thomas* by Georges de la Tour was purchased following a public subscription.

The Louvre now possesses a superb collection of French seventeenth-century painting representing all its different aspects. This richness has become even more apparent now that the huge works by Champaigne, Le Sueur, Le Brun and Poussin, which were confined to the reserve collection for so long, have finally been exhibited. However, even such a magnificent collection cannot hide the fact that there are still some gaps to be filled. The Louvre has no late work by Claude Lorrain for instance, nor a major piece by La Hyre. Similarly, with the exception of Valentin, the followers of Caravaggio barely figure, despite two important recent acquisitions, *The young singer* in 1966, one of Vignon's most successful paintings executed during his stay in Rome, and the colossal but rather unadventurous *Prince Marcantonio Doria* painted by Vouet in Genoa and presented to the Louvre in 1979.

The century that produced so many great still-life painters is still rather poorly represented, in spite of the recent acquisition of works by Dupuis, Linard and Stosskopf. Some of these painters may be lesser known, but opinions are changing constantly: nobody at the beginning of this century had heard of Georges de la Tour. Today more and more painters are gaining the recognition they deserve. It is imperative that the Louvre show all the varied aspects of French painting and offer the most complete image of the seventeenth century possible.

<
Claude Vignon
Tours, 1593 – Paris, 1670
*Solomon and the
Queen of Sheba*
1624

Canvas
80 x 119 cm
Purchased in 1933

v
Valentin de Boulogne
Coulommiers, 1594 –
Rome, 1632
*Concert with Roman
bas-relief*
Circa 1622/25

Canvas
173 x 214 cm
*Collection of Louis XV
Purchased in 1742*

The influence of Caravaggio's dramatic style which revolutionised European painting at the beginning of the seventeenth century can be seen clearly in Valentin's work. He would have come into contact with Caravaggio's work in Rome where he went as a very young man, and spent all of his short career. In The Judgement of Solomon the strength of forms outlined against the shadow, so reminiscent of Caravaggio, does not preclude an atmosphere of mystery and poetry that is peculiar to Valentin. Louis XIV owned several of his paintings; five are still hanging in the King's bedchamber in the Château de Versailles.

^
Valentin de Boulogne
Coulommiers, 1594 –
Rome, 1632
The judgement of Solomon
Circa 1625 (?)

Canvas
176 x 210 cm
Collection of Louis XIV
Purchased in 1661

>
Claude Vignon
Tours, 1593 –
Paris, 1670
The young singer
Circa 1622/23

Canvas
95 x 90 cm
*Presented by the Société
des Amis du Louvre, 1966*

∨
**Valentin de
Boulogne**
Coulommiers, 1594 –
Rome, 1632
The fortune-teller
Circa 1628

Canvas
125 x 175 cm
*Collection of Louis XIV
Purchased before 1683*

<
Nicolas Régnier
Maubeuge, 1591 –
Venice, 1667
The fortune-teller
Circa 1625

Canvas
127 x 150 cm
Purchased in 1816

v
Georges de la Tour
Vic-sur-Seille, 1593 –
Lunéville, 1652
Saint Thomas
Circa 1625-30

Canvas
69 x 61 cm
*Acquired in 1988
by national public
subscription*

The acquisition for the museum collections of the St Thomas, *one of La Tour's 'daylight' masterpieces, was the outcome of a vigorous campaign and a public fund to prevent the canvas from leaving France. The bold, simplified modelling is combined here with a psychological analysis of rare subtlety. The refined sable and slate-grey colouring distinguishes the work from the five other La Tours in the Louvre, where reds predominate.*

<
Georges de La Tour
Vic-sur-Seille, 1593 –
Lunéville, 1652
*The penitent Magdalen
with night-light,* called
The Terff Magdalen
Circa 1640/45 (?)

Canvas
128 x 94 cm
Purchased in 1949

*This painting was discovered in the church of Bois-Anzeray in
1945 and is almost certainly the canvas known to have been
given by the town of Lunéville to La Ferté, governor of
Lorraine at the end of 1649. It is the most complete and
ambitious of La Tour's night scenes, with the blue of the coat
reverberating in the range of warm tones, and is also one of
his last works. An old copy of good quality is in the museum
of Berlin-Dahlem.*

<

Georges de La Tour
Vic-sur-Seille, 1593 – Lunéville, 1652
The cheat
Circa 1635 (?)

Canvas. 106 x 146 cm
Purchased in 1972

∧

Georges de La Tour
Vic-sur-Seille, 1593 – Lunéville, 1652
St Sebastian tended by Irene
1649 (?)

Canvas. 167 x 131 cm
Presented by the Société des Amis du Louvre, 1979

<

Simon Vouet
Paris, 1590 – Paris, 1649
Prince Marcantonio Doria
1621

Canvas
129 x 95 cm
Anonymous gift, 1979

<

Simon Vouet
Paris, 1590 – Paris, 1649
Allegory of wealth
Circa 1630/35

Canvas
170 x 124 cm
Collection of Louis XIII

<<

Nicolas Tournier
Montbéliard, 1590 –
Toulouse (?), 1638/39
*Crucifixion with the Virgin,
St John and St Vincent
de Paul*
Circa 1635 (?)

Canvas
422 x 292 cm
*Exchanged with the Musée
de Toulouse in 1800*

>

Simon Vouet
Paris, 1590 – Paris, 1649
*The Presentation
in the Temple*
1641

Canvas
393 x 250 cm
*From the main altar of
the Jesuit church now
Saint Paul-Saint Louis, Paris
Collection of the Académie*

Poussin spent almost all his career in Rome painting in isolation. He endeavoured to create a clear visual language that would appeal to the spectator's mind and affect him rationally rather than through the emotions. His œuvre is one of the supreme expressions of classicism in French art. The subject of The inspiration of the poet *remains under discussion: it is possible that the young man on the right, being inspired by Apollo, is Virgil and the figure standing on the left Calliope, muse of epic poetry. In both figures there are direct references to antique sculpture, as so often in Poussin's work, and the golden light shows the influence of the great Venetian painters of the sixteenth century.*

<
Nicolas Poussin
Les Andelys, 1594 –
Rome, 1665
Self-portrait
1650

Canvas
92 x 74 cm
Purchased in 1797

v
Nicolas Poussin
Les Andelys, 1594 –
Rome, 1665
*The plague
at Ashdod*
1630

Canvas
148 x 198 cm
*Collection of Louis XIV
Purchased in 1665*

> **Nicolas Poussin**
Les Andelys, 1594 –
Rome, 1665
Echo and Narcissus
Circa 1628/30 (?)

Canvas
74 x 100 cm
Collection of Louis XIV
Purchased before 1683

v
Nicolas Poussin
Les Andelys, 1594 –
Rome, 1665
The inspiration of the poet
Circa 1630 (?)

Canvas
182.5 x 213 cm
Purchased in 1911

<

Nicolas Poussin
Les Andelys, 1594 –
Rome, 1665
*The institution
of the Eucharist*
1640

Canvas
325 x 250 cm
*Painted for the Sainte-Chapelle,
Saint-Germain-en-Laye
Collection of Louis XIII*

>

Nicolas Poussin
Les Andelys, 1594 –
Rome, 1665
Winter or *The Deluge*
Between 1660 and 1664

Canvas
118 x 160 cm
*One of a series of four paintings
depicting the seasons
Collection of Louis XIV
Purchased in 1665*

>
Claude Gellée,
called **Le Lorrain**
Chamagne, 1600 –
Rome, 1682
*The disembarkation
of Cleopatra at Tarsus*
Circa 1642/43

Canvas
119 x 170 cm
Collection of Louis XIV
Purchased before 1683

<
Claude Gellée,
called **Le Lorrain**
Chamagne, 1600 –
Rome, 1682
*Landscape with Paris and
Oenone,* called *The ford*
1648

Canvas
119 x 150 cm
*This painting is a pendant
to* Ulysses returns Chryseis
to her father
Collection of Louis XIV
Purchased in 1665

<
Claude Gellée,
called **Le Lorrain**
Chamagne, 1600 –
Rome, 1682
*Ulysses returns
Chryseis to her father*
1648 (?)

Canvas
119 x 150 cm
Collection of Louis XIV
Purchased in 1665

> **Laurent de La Hyre**
Paris, 1606 – Paris (?), 1656
*Laban searching Jacob's
baggage for the stolen idols*
1647

Canvas
95 x 133 cm
Collection of Louis XVI

> **Pierre Patel the Elder**
Picardy, circa 1605 –
Paris, 1676
Landscape with ruins
Circa 1646/47

Canvas
73 x 150 cm
*From the Cabinet de l'Amour
in the Hôtel Lambert, Paris
Collection of Louis XVI
Purchased in 1776*

∧ **François Perrier**
Saint-Jean-de-Losne (?)
Circa 1600 (?) – Paris 1650
*Aeneas and his companions
fighting the Harpies*
Circa 1646/47

Canvas
155 x 218 cm
*From the Cabinet de l'Amour
in the Hôtel Lambert, Paris
Collection of Louis XVI
Purchased in 1776*

> **Jacques Blanchard**
Paris, 1600 – Paris, 1638
*Venus and the three Graces
surprised by a mortal*
Circa 1631/33

Canvas
170 x 218 cm
Purchased in 1921

>
Jacques Stella
Lyons, 1596 – Paris, 1657
Minerva and the Muses
Circa 1640/5

Canvas
116 x 162 cm
Collection of Louis XIV

V
Philippe de Champaigne
Brussels, 1602 – Paris, 1674
*The miracles of
the penitent St Mary*
1656

Canvas
219 x 336 cm
*From the apartments of Anne
of Austria in the convent
of Val de Grâce, Paris
Seized during the French
Revolution*

>
Philippe de Champaigne
Brussels, 1602 –
Paris, 1674
Portrait of a man
1650

Canvas
91 x 72 cm
Purchased in 1906

v
Philippe de Champaigne
Brussels, 1602 –
Paris, 1674
The Ex-voto of 1662
1662

Canvas
165 x 229 cm
Seized during the French Revolution

>
Louis *or*
Antoine Le Nain
Laon, circa 1600/10 –
Paris, 1648
The peasant family
Circa 1640/45

Canvas
113 x 159 cm
Purchased in 1915

<
**Philippe de
Champaigne**
Brussels, 1602 –
Paris, 1674
*Portrait of Robert
Arnauld d'Andilly*
1667

Canvas
78 x 64 cm
*Given in lieu
of death duty, 1979*

v
Louis *or*
Antoine Le Nain
Laon, circa 1600/10 –
Paris, 1648
The haywain, also
called *The return
from hay-making*
1641

Canvas
56 x 76 cm
*Bequeathed by Vicomte Philippe
de Saint-Albin, 1879*

<
Sébastien Bourdon
Montpellier, 1616 –
Paris, 1671
The beggars
Circa 1635/40 (?)

Wood
49 x 65 cm
Royal Collection

v
**Louis *or*
Antoine Le Nain**
Laon, circa 1600/10 –
Paris, 1648
The group of smokers, also
called *The guard-room*
1643

Canvas
117 x 137 cm
Purchased in 1969

Lubin Baugin
Pithiviers, circa
1612 – Paris, 1663
*Still life with
wafer biscuits*
Circa 1630/35

Wood
41 x 52 cm
Purchased in 1954

Louise Moillon
Paris, 1610 –
Paris, 1696
*Cup of cherries
and melon*
1633

Wood
48 x 65 cm
*Given in lieu
of death duty, 1981*

∨
Pierre Dupuis
Monfort l'Amaury,
1610 – Paris, 1682
*Plums and peaches
on a table*
1650

Canvas
51 x 60 cm
*Given in lieu
of death duty, 1981*

∧

Eustache Le Sueur
Paris, 1617 – Paris, 1655
Group portrait, called
A gathering of friends
Circa 1640/42

Canvas
127 x 195 cm
Collection of Louis XVI

∨

Eustache Le Sueur
Paris, 1617 – Paris, 1655
*St Gervase and St Protase
brought before Anastasius
for refusing to sacrifice
to Jupiter*
Commissioned in 1652

Canvas
357 x 684 cm
*Cartoon for the tapestry
in Saint Gervais, Paris
Seized during the French Revolution*

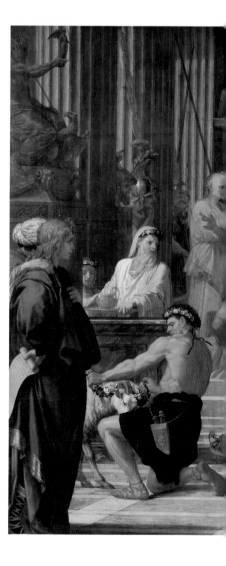

∨

Mathieu (?) Le Nain
Laon, circa 1608/10 –
Paris, 1677
The supper at Emmaus
Circa 1645 (?)

Canvas
75 x 92 cm
Purchased in 1950

> **Eustache Le Sueur**
Paris, 1617 – Paris, 1655
*Three muses: Melpomene,
Erato and Polyhymnia*
Circa 1652/55

Wood
130 x 130 cm
*From the Chambre des Muses
in the Hôtel Lambert, Paris
Collection of Louis XVI
Purchased in 1776*

<
Sébastien Bourdon
Montpellier, 1616 –
Paris, 1671
*A scene from Roman history
(Antony and Cleopatra?)*
Circa 1645 (?)

Canvas
145 x 197 cm
*Presented by the Société
des Amis du Louvre, 1979*

v
Charles Le Brun
Paris, 1619 – Paris, 1690
Alexander and Porus
Exhibited at the Salon
of 1673

Canvas
470 x 1264 cm
Collection of Louis XIV

>
Charles Le Brun
Paris, 1619 – Paris, 1690
Pietà
Between 1643/45

Canvas
146 x 222 cm
*Seized during
the French Revolution*

∧
Charles Le Brun
Paris,1619 – Paris, 1690
Chancellor Séguier
Circa 1655/57

Canvas
295 x 351 cm
*Purchased in 1942,
with the help of the Société
des Amis du Louvre*

*This portrait of Chancellor Séguier in his state robes in a solemn
work yet one in which each has been portrayed with a warm
humanity. It shows the Chancellor in an official cortege, perhaps
entering a town. Le Brun's range of copper and blue slate hues
are particularly discreet and refined in this work.*

>
Pierre Mignard
Troyes, 1612 – Paris, 1695
The Virgin of the grapes
Circa 1640/50 (?)

Canvas
121 x 94 cm
Collection of Louis XIV

∨
Charles Le Brun
Paris, 1619 – Paris, 1690
*The Adoration
of the shepherds*
1689

Canvas
151 x 213 cm
Collection of Louis XIV

The end of Louis XIV's reign and the Regency

The transition from the painting of the end of Louis XIV's reign to that of the Regency was from one of pomp and celebrity, to one of delicate dreamlike elegance.

Rigaud's *Louis XIV* and Watteau's *Pilgrimage to Cythera* each seem to typify the mood of the century in which they were produced; the first by its ostentation and solemnity, the second by its refined and dreamy elegance, although only sixteen years separate them. For a long time French painting of around 1700 was deemed to be uninteresting, academic and too much influenced by the taste of the court. Now, after recent art historical research and new evaluation of the work of Rubens and Titian, the variety and creativity of this period are appreciated, and it is interesting, despite the difference in generations, to consider La Fosse, Jouvenet, Coypel, Rigaud and Largillière with the younger Watteau and Lemoyne (both of whom died young), since all acknowledge their debt to the rich and supple execution of Flemish painters and the delightful colour ranges used by the Venetians.

Most of the decorative works commissioned by Louis XIV still adorn, or have now been returned to, the palaces for which they were executed but some works by Coypel, La Fosse and Desportes from the royal collection are now in the Louvre. Paintings depicting the King's victories by Van der Meulen or Parrocel were also part of the royal collection and are now in the Louvre, as is the portrait of the King by Rigaud, a symbol of the French monarchy. The canvas had been intended as a gift for Philip V of Spain, Louis XIV's grandson, but on seeing the painting the King liked it so much that he decided to keep it and had a replica made to send to Madrid. During Louis XV's reign the collection acquired other paintings, for example, Rigaud bequeathed his last work, *The Presentation in the Temple,* which owes so much to Rembrandt, to the King. Louis XVI still bought Coypels, Van der Meulens and he bought one canvas by Louis de Boulogne. But by then the taste for works of Louis XIV's period and that of the Regency was out of fashion and it was not until the Revolution that new paintings came into the collection: three little works by Lemoyne seized from the nobility and above all the fine series of Jouvenet's work from Parisian churches. During the Restoration Rigaud's portrait of *Bossuet* and Jouvenet's portrait of *Dr Raymond Finot* were purchased, the latter because it was thought to be of Fagon, Louis XIV's doctor.

With the Académie collection, which entered the Louvre during the Revolution, came a number of Académie election paintings, many of which are masterpieces: Rigaud's portrait of *Desjardins* executed in 1692 for his acceptance in 1700, Largillière's portrait of *Le Brun* (1686), Desportes' *Self portrait as a huntsman* (1699), Santerre's *Susanna bathing* and Pater's *Fête champêtre* (1728). But the most important of these was the *Pilgrimage to Cythera,* Watteau's most popular painting and for a long time the only one by him in the Louvre. In the Académie's collection were other important paintings such as Rigaud's *Portrait of the artist's mother from two different angles* bequeathed to the Académie by the painter, and Jouvenet's *The Descent from the Cross.*

Of very great importance to the Louvre was the bequest of the La Caze collection in 1869. Dr Louis La Caze, a painter himself, was a keen collector of well-executed pictures with vigorous brushwork, and therefore favoured works from a period influenced by Titian, Rubens and Rembrandt. His taste can be seen in the *Democritus* by Antoine Coypel and in *Hercules and Omphale* by Lemoyne. The breadth and quality of collections of works by certain artists in the Louvre is entirely due to the generosity of La Caze. For example, he bequeathed six works by Largillière, including the *Family portrait* originally thought to be of the artist himself and his family, and many works by Pater and Watteau. La Caze's eight Watteaus, including *The judgement of Paris* and *Giles,* which had belonged to Vivant Denon, Director of the Musée Napoléon, meant that this most poetic of French painters was at last fairly well represented in the Louvre.

Since then, acquisitions from this period have been rare: a few works by Largillière have been given or bequeathed and a couple of theatrical subjects by Gillot were purchased in 1923 and 1945. Two rare silvery Lancrets, *The seat of justice in the Parliament of Paris* and the *Presentation of the order of the Holy Spirit,* were purchased in 1949 and a small landscape by Watteau in 1937. More recently, three unusual works by Largillière were acquired, a small *Landscape* in 1971, the large, theatrical *Decorative composition* in 1979 and, most recently, one of his rare religious pieces. But, most importantly, the collection of paintings by Watteau – an artist who, despite La Caze, is still rather poorly represented here – has been augmented with the *Portrait of a gentleman, Diana bathing* and the tiny masterpiece, *Two cousins,* purchased in 1990. The opening of the new rooms in the Cour Carrée has enabled us to present a more complete display of paintings from this period. Jouvenet's huge glowing compositions, notably *The miraculous draught of fishes* and *The rising of Lazarus,* both painted in 1706 for the church of Saint-Nicholas-des-Champs in Paris, reveal an aspect of painting during Watteau's time that is not as yet well enough known.

∧
Charles de La Fosse
Paris, 1636 – Paris, 1716
The rescue of the infant Moses by Pharaoh's daughter
Commissioned in 1701

Canvas
125 x 110 cm
Collection of Louis XIV

∧∧
Adam Frans van der Meulen
Brussels, 1632 – Paris, 1690
The defeat of the Spanish army near Bruges canal, 1667
Circa 1670 (?)

Canvas
50 x 80 cm
Collection of Louis XIV

>
Joseph Parrocel
Brignoles, 1646 – Paris, 1704
The Crossing of the Rhine by the army of Louis XIV, 1672
1699

Canvas
234 x 164 cm
Collection of Louis XIV

This bold and vigorous painting, with its magnificent harmony of warm colours, foreshadows the most beautiful of the nineteenth-century Romantic paintings. Executed for the church of the Capuchins in the Place Louis-le-grand, Paris, it was donated to the Académie Royale de Peinture et de Sculpture in 1756. During the French Revolution it was acquired by the Louvre, as were all the other paintings which had belonged to the Académie.

∧
Jean Jouvenet
Rouen, 1644 – Paris, 1717
The Descent from the Cross
1697

Canvas
424 x 312 cm
Collection of the Académie

>
Hyacinthe Rigaud
Perpignan, 1659 – Paris, 1743
*Portrait of the artist's
mother from two
different angles*
1695

Canvas
83 x 103 cm
Collection of the Académie

∧
Jean Jouvenet
Rouen, 1644 – Paris, 1717
Dr Raymond Finot
Exhibited at the Salon
of 1704

Canvas
73 x 59 cm
Purchased in 1838

>
Hyacinthe Rigaud
Perpignan, 1659 – Paris, 1743
Louis XIV, King of France
1701

Canvas
277 x 194 cm
Collection of Louis XIV

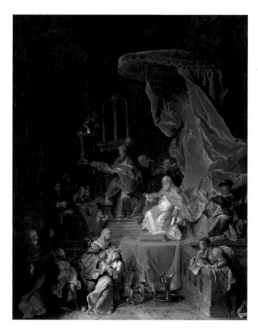

<

Hyacinthe Rigaud
Perpignan, 1659 – Paris, 1743
The Presentation in the Temple
1743

Wood
83 x 68 cm
Collection of Louis XV

∨

Antoine Coypel
Paris, 1661 – Paris, 1722
The swooning of Esther
Exhibited at the Salon of 1704

Canvas
105 x 137 cm
Collection of Louis XIV

∧

Antoine Coypel
Paris, 1661 – Paris, 1722
Democritus. 1692

Canvas. 69 x 57 cm
Bequeathed by Louis La Caze, 1869

<

Nicolas de Largillière
Paris, 1656 – Paris, 1746
Decorative composition
Circa 1720/30 (?)

Canvas. 261 x 253 cm
Purchased in 1979

∨
Nicolas de Largillière
Paris, 1656 – Paris, 1746
Study of hands
Circa 1715

Canvas
65 x 52 cm
Deposited by the Musée des
Beaux-Arts, Algiers, 1970

∧
Nicolas de Largillière
Paris, 1656 – Paris, 1746
Family portrait
Circa 1710 (?)

Canvas
149 x 200 cm
Bequeathed by Louis La Caze, 1869

∧
Claude Gillot
Langres, 1673 – Paris, 1722
The two coaches
Circa 1710 (?)

Canvas. 127 x 160 cm
Purchased in 1923

<
Jean-Baptiste Santerre
Magny-en-Vexin, 1658 – Paris, 1717
Susanna bathing
1704

Canvas. 205 x 145 cm
Collection of the Académie

<
Jean Antoine Watteau
Valenciennes, 1684 –
Nogent-sur Marne, 1721
The judgement of Paris
Circa 1720 (?)

Wood
47 x 31 cm
Bequeathed by Louis La Caze, 1869

∨
Jean Antoine Watteau
Valenciennes, 1684 –
Nogent-sur-Marne, 1721
The pilgrimage to Cythera
1717

Canvas
129 x 194 cm
Collection of the Académie

It was with this painting, called at that time The pilgrimage to Cythera, *that Watteau was officially accepted by the Académie Royale de Peinture et de Sculpture in 1717. The title* The departure for Cythera *under which it became famous is in fact incorrect as the pilgrims are already on the Island of Venus and are preparing to leave. The subject was inspired by Rubens'* Garden of love. *The open, curving composition, the clear colours and general mood of both happiness and nostalgia, were to be important influences on French eighteenth-century painting.*

∨
Nicolas Lancret
Paris, 1690 – Paris, 1743
Winter
1738

Canvas
69 x 89 cm
Collection of Louis XV

∧
Nicolas Lancret
Paris, 1690 – Paris, 1743
*The seat of justice in the
Parliament of Paris (1723)*
Circa 1724 (?)

Canvas
56 x 81.5 cm
Purchased in 1949

∧
Jean Antoine Watteau
Valenciennes, 1684 –
Nogent-sur-Marne, 1721
Two cousins
Circa 1716

Canvas. 30 x 36 cm
Purchased in 1990

>
Jean Antoine Watteau
Valenciennes, 1684 –
Nogent-sur-Marne, 1721
Portrait of a gentleman
Circa 1715/20

Canvas. 130 x 97 cm
Purchased in 1973

^
Jean Antoine Watteau
Valenciennes, 1684 – Nogent-sur-Marne, 1721
Gilles, circa 1718/20 (?)

Canvas. 184.5 x 149.5 cm
Bequeathed by Louis La Caze, 1869

^
Jean Restout
Rouen, 1692 – Paris, 1768
Pentecost, 1732

Canvas. 465 x 778 cm

^
Jean-Baptiste Pater
Valenciennes, 1695 – Paris, 1736
The Chinese hunt, 1736

Canvas. 55 x 46 cm
*Presented by the Office des Biens
Privés, 1950*

<
François Lemoyne
Paris, 1688 – Paris, 1737
Hercules and Omphale, 1724

Canvas. 184 x 149 cm
Bequeathed by Louis La Caze, 1869

The mid-eighteenth century

This period so highly considered today has long been underestimated and badly represented in the Louvre. The blame for this lies squarely with Louis XV's omission to collect the works of his own times.

On the other hand, during his reign sovereigns from the rest of Europe were voraciously buying contemporary French paintings: Frederick II of Prussia acquired the Watteaus, Lancrets and Chardins which today are the glory of Charlottenburg; his sister Louise-Ulrique of Sweden, well advised by her French ambassador Tessin, purchased the finest Bouchers and Chardins; Catherine the Great, Empress of Russia, bought the entire collection belonging to Louis-Antoine Crozat, Baron de Thiers, after his death in 1770. Comprising important paintings from all periods, the Crozat collection also included contemporary works. Louis XV, on the other hand, did not own a single painting by Watteau or Fragonard. He did, however, commission a number of paintings to hang over doors: still lifes from Chardin, such as the *Attributes of the Arts* and the *Attributes of Music* for the Château de Choisy, and from Lancret *The four seasons* for the Château de la Muette. For the Château de Fontainebleau he commissioned Van Loo's *The halt during the hunt* and Parrocel's *The halt of the grenadiers.* Many of the Bouchers, and the only Fragonard, *Chaereas and Callirrhoe,* purchased during Louis XV's reign were tapestry cartoons and not easel paintings. Nevertheless, he did buy two of Chardin's most beautiful works at the Salon of 1740, *The diligent mother* and *Saying grace.* Also, the Marquis de Marigny, Surintendant des Bâtiments from 1751 to 1774, commissioned some large series which cannot be overlooked. One example of these is the group of fifteen large paintings depicting *The ports of France,* commissioned from Joseph Vernet in 1753 and completed in 1765. Today, except for the two in the Louvre, this series is in the Musée de la Marine.

Louis XVI seems to have been scarcely more fond of contemporary painting than his grandfather but did purchase works by Subleyras, Carle Van Loo and Raoux, the most refined and restrained of eighteenth-century artists. He bought Greuze's already popular *The village bride* in 1782 at the sale following the death of the Marquis de Marigny, and commissioned Hubert Robert to paint the four large *Antiquities of France* for the Château de Fontainebleau.

Among works seized during the Revolution were six paintings by Subleyras from the Comte d'Angiviller, the Comte de Pestre Senef and the Duc de Penthièvre among others; and several landscapes by Joseph Vernet from the Comtesse du Barry, the Duchesse de Noailles and Boutin, Treasurer of the Navy. Two works by Vien and,

The broken jug by Greuze, one of his sentimental works which was highly regarded at the time, were also seized from the Comtesse du Barry. The Académie collection contained many important canvases of this period: election pieces by Boucher, *Renaud and Armide* (1734), Chardin, *The skate* and *The buffet,* Tocqué, portraits of *Galloche* and *Lemoyne* (1734); portraits of *Oudry* and *Adam* (1753) by Perronneau and *Septimus Severus* (1769) by Greuze. Many works by Restout were taken from the churches and convents in Paris. A rare example of a French painting 'captured' abroad and subsequently left in the Louvre was Subleyras' vast *Christ in the house of Simon* which came from the convent of Asti near Turin to join the sketch for it which has been acquired by Louis XVI twelve years earlier. Subleyras (once again a 'Roman'), author of austere but delicate works, was one of the only painters from the first half of the eighteenth century to be appreciated during the neo-classical period. Not until the mid-nineteenth century was much interest taken in artists of Louis XV's reign, their work being considered frivolous and dissolute. Greuze, one aspect of whose work was serious and much concerned with virtue, was not scorned in quite the same way and the pair that complete *The father's curse, The ungrateful son* and *The punished son,* were purchased in 1820.

The gift of Fragonard's *Music Lesson* in 1849 heralds a change in taste; *The inquisitive girls* by the same artist formed part of the Sauvageot gift in 1856. Chardin was now particularly appreciated and seven of his works were bought during the Second Empire, before the La Caze bequest, which was to form the major part of the Louvre's collection of mid-eighteenth-century French painting. With this bequest came the paintings that Louis XV and Louis XVI had not appreciated: thirteen major works by Chardin including *Still life with jar of olives, The copper drinking fountain* and *The silver goblet;* nine sparkling Fragonards, among them *The bathers* and four imaginary figures; four Bouchers and several paintings by De Troy, Tocqué, Hubert Robert, Raoux, Nattier and Greuze. These beautiful works, which quickly became favourites with the public were largely responsible for the general impression that the eighteenth century produced only small and charming paintings. La Caze's taste for these vigorous seductive works, canvases executed for collectors and avidly bought by them, even today tends to divert us from fully understanding the eighteenth century's ambitions towards 'la grande peinture', paintings depicting subjects of morality and history.

The Louvre's collection continued to grow with purchases and bequests following on La Caze. Chardin's portraits of the Godefroy children, *Child with a top* and *Young man with a violin,* were purchased in 1907 and soon became popular; Boucher's *The afternoon meal* and the Louvre's most beautiful Nattier, *Comtesse Tessin,* were bequeathed in 1895 by Dr Achille Malécot; Chardin's *Portrait of Aved* was bequeathed by Paul Bureau in 1915; and several Greuzes were bequeathed by Baronne Nathaniel and Baron Arthur de Rothschild in 1899 and 1904. The bequest in 1915 of Baron Basile de Schlichting included works by Fragonard, Greuze, Nattier and Drouais.

Among more recent acquisitions the Carlos de Beistegui gift in 1942 contributed some important paintings: Fragonard's *Nude with cherubs* and an *Imaginary figure;* the most refined of Drouais, *Madame Drouais, wife of the artist;* and a large work by Nattier, *The Duchesse De Chaulnes as Hébé.* The Sommier gift included Chardin's marvellous white and turquoise *The young draughtsman sharpening his pencil,* the Péreire gift contained one of Vernet's most beautiful Italian scenes, *View of Naples,* which was later joined by its pair, another view of the same subject, and the Lyon gift (1961) contributed, amongst others, canvases by Robert and Vernet.

The most notable among recent acquisitions is the purchase of the famous *The bolt,* one of the key pictures in Fragonard's late work. More modest but nevertheless of great value are Subleyras' portrait of *Don Cesare Benvenuti,* Delaporte's *Still life with a carafe of barley wine,* and a youthful sketch by Boucher, which was bought in 1977, *Rebecca receiving Abraham's presents.* Among generous gifts should be mentioned the portrait of *Philippe Coypel* by his brother, Charles Antoine Coypel (Cailleux gift, 1968); Barbault's *The priest* and *The sultan* (François Heim gift, 1971); Dandré-Bardon's *Birth* (Benito Pardo gift, 1972); and Fragonard's *White bull* (Elaine and Michel David-Weill gift, 1976).

Thanks to the law which has been passed recently allowing the presentation of works of art in lieu of death duties, the Louvre's collection has gained three works which typify eighteenth-century France: Fragonard's portraits of the philosopher, *Diderot* (received in 1974) and the famous dancer, *Marie-Madeleine Guimard,* and Chardin's *Still life with dead hare* (received in 1979). The policy of collecting views of the Louvre, which was originated by Hubert Robert, Director in the eighteenth century, should be mentioned. One painting was given by Maurice Fenaille in 1912, ten others have been purchased or given since 1946–interior and exterior, real and imaginary. The highlight of this project came in 1975 with the purchase of two large paintings that had been exhibited at the Salon of 1796, *Project for the redecoration of the Grande Galerie* and *Imaginary view of the Grande Galerie in ruins,* both of which had for many years been in the Russian imperial collection in the palace of Tsarskoe-Selo.

Among the recent acquisitions, mention must be made of Chardin's *The canary, A Hunting meal* by J.F. de Troy which, like Fragonard's *The beggar's dream,* was given in lieu of death duties, and *The adoration of the shepherds,* also by Fragonard, which has rejoined its companion piece *The bolt.*

Let us not forget the Louvre's collection of pastels, unique both in number and quality, which was built up from the royal collection and that of the Académie française and added to over the years. The place in French pictorial art of these portraits 'painted in pastels' should not be underestimated. The collection of works by Quentin de La Tour, Perroneau and Chardin, especially, are without equal. A selection of the most beautiful of these pastels is now displayed in the Colonnade rooms on the second floor of the Cour Carrée.

While the Louvre's collection of eighteenth-century paintings rightly enjoy great prestige and are being added to regularly, there are nevertheless gaps that need filling. Few preliminary sketches, for example, which are one of the most attractive features of this period, have been acquired. Finally, let us stress once more the importance of displaying the large-scale pieces, facilitated by the opening of the rooms on the second floor of the Cour Carrée in 1992. At the turn of the century virtually all the French paintings of the eighteenth century could be seen displayed in one of the huge rooms now devoted to the nineteenth century. Small, medium and large, they were all hung cheek by jowl in three rows! Such a jumble would be inconceivable today, yet it remains our duty to exhibit the most important of the large-scale works and to display once more de Troy and Restout next to Chardin and Fragonard.

<
François Boucher
Paris, 1703 – Paris, 1770
Diana bathing
1742

Canvas
56 x 73 cm
Purchased in 1852

v
François Boucher
Paris, 1703 – Paris, 1770
The forest
1740

Canvas
131 x 163 cm
*Presented by the Office
des Biens Privés, 1951*

This subject was often treated by Boucher, and the Louvre has three other versions. The delightful and decorative design, full of light and charm, was woven for the series of tapestries The loves of the gods, *and typifies the spirit of Rococo decoration.*

^
François Boucher
Paris, 1703 – Paris, 1770
Vulcan presenting Venus with arms for Aeneas
1757

Canvas
320 x 320 cm
Tapestry cartoon for the Gobelins factor Collection of Louis XV

<
Carle Van Loo
Nice, 1705 – Paris, 1765
Aeneas carrying Anchises
1729

Canvas
110 x 105 cm
Collection of Louis XVI

∨
Carle Van Loo
Nice, 1705 – Paris, 1765
The halt during the hunt
1737

Canvas
220 x 250 cm
Collection of Louis XV

>
Jean-Baptiste Oudry
Paris, 1686 – Beauvais, 1755
Still life with pheasant
1753

Canvas
97 x 64 cm
*Presented by the Office
des Biens Privés, 1950*

∧
Jean François de Troy
Paris, 1679 – Rome, 1752
A Hunting Meal
1737

Canvas
241 x 170 cm
Given in lieu of death duties, 1990

>
Pierre Subleyras
Saint-Gilles-du-Gard, 1699 – Rome, 1749
Charon ferrying the Shades
Circa 1735/40(?)

Canvas
135 x 83 cm
*Seized during the French Revolution from
the collection of the Duc de Penthièvre*

∨

Pierre Subleyras
Saint-Gilles, 1699 –
Rome 1749
*Portrait, believed to be
of Giuseppe Baretti*
Circa 1745

Canvas
74 x 61 cm
*Presented by the Foundation
Bella et André Meyer, 1981*

∧
Jean Siméon Chardin
Paris, 1699 –
Paris, 1779
*Portrait of the artist
Jacques André
Joseph Aved*
1734

Canvas
138 x 105 cm
*Bequeathed by Paul
Bureau, 1915*

>
Jean Siméon Chardin
Paris, 1699 –
Paris, 1779
The diligent mother
Exhibited at the Salon
of 1740

Canvas
49 x 39 cm
Collection of Louis XV

<
Pierre Subleyras
Saint-Gilles-du-Gard,
1699 – Rome, 1749
Don Cesare Benvenuti
1742

Canvas
138 x 101 cm
Purchased in 1969

∨
Pierre Subleyras
Saint-Gilles-du-Gard,
1699 – Rome, 1749
*Christ's visit to
the house of Simon
the Pharisee*
1737

Canvas
215 x 679 cm
*From the Convent at Asti,
1799*

∧
Jean Siméon Chardin
Paris, 1699 – Paris, 1779
The Skate
1728

Canvas
114 x 146 cm
Collection of the Académie française

>
Jean Siméon Chardin
Paris, 1699 – Paris, 1779
The buffet
1728

Canvas
194 x 129 cm
Collection of the Académie

>
Jean Siméon Chardin
Paris, 1699 – Paris, 1779
*The young draughtsman
sharpening his pencil*
1737

Canvas
80 x 65 cm
*Presented by Madame Edmé
Sommier, 1943*

<
Jean Siméon Chardin
Paris, 1699 – Paris, 1799
Pipe and drinking glasses,
also called *La tabagie*
(The group of smokers)
Circa 1737

Canvas
32 x 42 cm
Purchased in 1867

v
Jean Siméon Chardin
Paris, 1699 – Paris, 1779
Still life with jar of olives
1760

Canvas
71 x 98 cm
Bequeathed by Louis La Caze, 1869

<
Jean Siméon Chardin
Paris, 1699 – Paris, 1779
The copper drinking fountain
Circa 1734

Wood
28,5 x 23 cm
Bequeathed by Louis La Caze, 1869

v
Roland Delaporte
Paris, 1724 – Paris, 1793
Still life with a carafe of barley wine,
called *'La petite collation'*
1787

Canvas
37,5 x 46 cm
Purchased in 1979

Commissioned for the king by Le Normant de Tournehem, the
Director of Buildings, and exhibited in the Salon of 1751, The Canary
subsequently became part of the collection of the Marquis de
Marigny, Madame de Pompadour's brother. One of Chardin's last
genre scenes, it shows the painter influenced by Dutch art, using a
detailed language and a delicate balance of light.

∧
Jean-Siméon Chardin
Paris, 1699 – Paris, 1779
The Canary
1750-51

Canvas
50 x 43 cm
Purchased in 1985

∧

Jean-Baptiste Perronneau
Paris, 1715 – Amsterdam, 1783
Madame de Sorquainville, 1749

Canvas. 101 x 81 cm
Presented by D. David Weill, 1937

<

Jean-Marc Nattier
Paris, 1685 – Paris, 1766
Comtesse Tessin
1741

Canvas
81 x 65 cm
Bequeathed by
Dr Achille Malécot, 1895

>

François-Hubert Drouais
Paris, 1727 – Paris, 1775
Madame Drouais,
wife of the artist
Circa 1758

Canvas
82.5 x 62 cm
Bequeathed by Carlos
de Beistegui, 1942

∧

Charles-Antoine Coypel
Paris, 1694 – Paris, 1752
Philippe Coypel,
brother of the artist
1732

Canvas
75 x 61 cm
Presented by Jean Cailleux
and Denise Cailleux, 1968

>

Louis Tocqué
Paris, 1696 – Paris, 1772
Marie Leczinska,
Queen of France
1740

Canvas
277 x 191 cm
Collection of Louis XV

<
Joseph Vernet
Avignon, 1714 – Paris, 1789
View of Naples
1748

Canvas
100 x 198 cm
Presented by André Péreire, 1949

Jean-Baptiste Greuze
Tournus, 1725 – Paris, 1805
The village bride
Exhibited at the Salon
of 1761

Canvas
92 x 117 cm
Collection of Louis XVI
Purchased in 1782

v
Joseph Vernet
Avignon, 1714 – Paris, 1789
*The town and harbour
of Toulon*
1756

Canvas
165 x 263 cm
Collection of Louis XV

>
Jean-Baptiste Greuze
Tournus, 1725 – Paris, 1805
Self-portrait
Circa 1785

Canvas
73 x 59 cm
Purchased in 1820

∨
Jean-Baptiste Greuze
Tournus, 1725 – Paris, 1805
The punished son
1778

Canvas
130 x 163 cm
Purchased in 1820

Nicolas Bernard Lépicié
Paris, 1735 – Paris, 1784
*The young draughtsman,
Carle Vernet, aged fourteen*
1772

Canvas
41 x 33 cm
*Bequeathed by Horace
Paul Delaroche, 1890*

∧
Joseph Siffred Duplessis
Carpentras, 1725 –
Versailles, 1802
*Christophe Gabriel
Allegrain, sculptor*
1774

Canvas
130 x 97 cm
Collection of the Académie

Jean-Baptiste Greuze
Tournus, 1725 – Paris, 1805
*Portrait of
Claude-Henri Watelet*
1763

Canvas
115 x 88 cm
Given in lieu of death duty, 1981

It was thanks to this painting that Fragonard was accepted by the Académie as a 'history painter'. He was soon to abandon this type of subject-matter and devote himself to the pleasant, often frivolous, paintings for which he is famous. The movement in the composition, the sense of drama and the strong light effects seen here are all in the best tradition of Italian Baroque painting.

V

Jean Honoré Fragonard
Grasse, 1732 – Paris, 1806
*The high priest Chaereas
sacrificing himself
for Callirrhoe*
1765

Canvas
309 x 400 cm
*Tapestry cartoon for the Gobelins
factory (never executed)*
Collection of Louis XV

^

Jean-Honoré Fragonard
Grasse, 1732 – Paris, 1806
*The Adoration
of the Shepherds*
Circa 1775

Canvas
73 x 93 cm
*Gift of M and Mme Robetto Polo,
1988*

<

Jean Honoré Fragonard
Grasse, 1732 – Paris, 1806
The storm
1759 (?)

Canvas
73 x 97 cm
*Bequeathed by Louis La Caze,
1869*

>
Jean Honoré Fragonard
Grasse, 1732 – Paris, 1806
The bathers
Circa 1772/75

Canvas
64 x 80 cm
Bequeathed by Louis La Caze,
1869

v
Jean Honoré Fragonard
Grasse, 1732 – Paris, 1806
The bolt
Circa 1778

Canvas
73 x 93 cm
Purchased in 1974

<
Jean Honoré Fragonard
Grasse, 1732 – Paris, 1806
*Marie-Madeleine Guimard,
dancer*
Circa 1769

Canvas
81.5 x 65 cm
*Presented in lieu
of death duties, 1974*

∨
Noël Hallé
Paris, 1711 – Paris, 1781
*The Race between
Hippomenes and Atalanta*
1762-65

Canvas
321 x 712 cm
Collection of Louis XV

> **Hubert Robert**
Paris, 1733 – Paris, 1808
Imaginary view of the
Grande Galerie
in the Louvre in ruins
Exhibited at the Salon of 1796

Canvas
114.5 x 146 cm
Purchased in 1975

v **Hubert Robert**
Paris, 1733 – Paris, 1808
The Pont du Gard
Exhibited at the Salon of 1787

Canvas
242 x 242 cm
Collection of Louis XVI

The neo-classical period

Neo-classical painting in the Louvre, particularly the collection of the works of David, demonstrates dramatically the development of the style from the reign of Louis XVI to the Revolution. The quality of the collection is key to the contemporary re-assessment of the achievement of neo-classical painting.

Painting labelled 'neo-classical' was often thought to be cold and devoid of any true creativity, but recent exhibitions and publications have shown that it was, in fact, an extremely lively period, full of contradictions and rich in artistic personalities. French artists, above all Jacques Louis David, were the leaders of this European movement and no other museum can show the origins and development of neo-classical painting in France so comprehensively.

During Louis XVI's reign the policy of encouraging the painting of historical subjects, maintained by the Comte d'Angiviller, Surintendant des Bâtiments, meant that the King commissioned or purchased large paintings, often of Greek or Roman subjects destined to be woven as tapestries, several of which are still in the Louvre. The Direction des Bâtiments du Roi purchased two canvases by David which exploded upon the art scene and revolutionised painting of the period. These were *The oath of the Horatii* and *Brutus*, which stunned public and artists alike with their new plasticity and emotive power. At this time also Regnault's masterpiece of tortured elegance, *The Descent from the Cross*, which had been commissioned as an altar-piece for the chapel at the Château de Fontainebleau, was purchased.

During the Revolution the government purchased a number of works that had been commissioned during the Monarchy, while paintings such as David's *Combat between Minerva and Mars* (second Prix de Rome in 1771) and Regnault's *Education of Achilles* (1782), were acquired with the Académie collection. Peyron's *The Funeral of Miltiades* and Madame Vigée-Lebrun's *Self-portrait with daughter* were among those seized from the Comte d'Angiviller, Gauffier's *Jacob and Laban's daughters* was seized from the Bernard collection, and David's signed copy of *Belisarius* from the Duchesse de Noailles.

During the Empire huge paintings of contemporary history were commissioned to glorify the Napoleonic era: David's *The Consecration of the Emperor Napoleon and Coronation of the Empress Josephine,* and Gros' *Bonaparte visiting the plague-stricken at Jaffa* and *Napoleon on the battlefield of Eylau.* The last two demonstrate the first important signs of the Romantic sensibility that was to pervade nineteenth-century Europe.

<
Marie-Guillemine Benoist
Paris, 1768 –
Paris, 1826
Portrait of a negress
Exhibited (under this title)
at the Salon of 1800

Canvas
81 x 65 cm
Purchased in 1818

Nearly all the important acquisitions of 'la grande peinture' of the neo-classical period came after the Restoration, when in 1818 the Musée de Luxembourg was created exclusively for the work of living artists and a deliberate acquisitions policy was established. Girodet's *The Deluge, The entombment of Atala* and *The sleep of Endymion* were bought in 1818, the large works by Guérin were bought between 1817 and 1830, except for *Phaedra and Hippolytus* which was bought at the Salon of 1802, Gerard's *Cupid and Psyche* was bought in 1822 and in 1826 Prud'hon's *Justice and Divine Vengeance pursuing Crime,* executed for the Palais de Justice, was assigned to the Louvre by the City of Paris. In 1819 *The Sabine women* and *Leonidas at Thermopylae* were bought indirectly from David, by then in exile in Brussels. In 1823 the Comte d'Artois presented the painting of *Paris and Helen* that he had commissioned and purchased from David before the upheaval of the Revolution, and an unfinished masterpiece, the portrait of *Madame Récamier* was bought at the sale of David's studio in 1826, the year after his death.

In the second half of the nineteenth century portraits were the main contribution to the Louvre's collection of neo-classical art, often given or bequeathed by the artists' descendants, or by the sitters or their families. Two of Madame Vigée-Lebrun's masterpieces, another *Self-portrait* and the portrait of *Hubert Robert,* full of fire and tension, were donated in 1843 by Madame Tripier-Le Franc, niece of the artist. David's portraits of *Monsieur Pécoul* and *Madame Pécoul* were acquired the next year and, in 1852, the artist Eugéne Isabey presented a fine Gérard, the portrait of his father *Jean-Baptiste Isabey* and David's *Self-portrait*. In 1855 Madame Mongez bequeathed a douple portrait by David of herself and her husband; David's *Madame Trudaine* was given in 1890 by Horace Paul Delaroche; and Gros'*Christine Boyer,* Lucien Bonaparte's first wife, was acquired in 1894.

The twentieth century has added little to this exceptional collection, but the clear and fresh images of *Monsieur Sériziat* and *Madame Sériziat* by David were purchased in 1902. Acquisitions of note during this period are Prud'hon's *Young Zephyr* in the Schlichting bequest of 1915, David's only landscape, the exquisite *View of the Luxembourg gardens,* a gift of Bernheim-Jeune in 1912, and above all the Comte d'Espine's splendid collection given by his daughter, the Princesse de Croy, in 1930. The main feature of this collection was the group of landscapes painted in the open air by Michallon (27 works) and, more importantly, by Valenciennes (127 works).

In the last fifty years or so more fine portraits have been acquired: *Madame de Verninac, Monsieur Meyer* and *General Bonaparte* by David, *Madame Lecerf* by Gérard (Beistegui bequest, 1942) and *Madame Pasteur* by Gros (Pasteur gift, 1948). In order to represent the whole range of neo-classical art a number of purchases have also been made recently: Guérin's *Shepherds at the tomb of Amyntas,* the subtle *Still life with flowers* by the Lyonnais artist, Berjon, in 1974, and Regnault's *Socrates and Alcibiades* in 1976. The most recent acquisitions of rare works include Prud'hon's *Portrait of the King of Rome,* a beautiful Roman landscape by Granet and the *Portrait of the young Romainville-Trioson* by Girodet.

This aim of covering the whole period in depth should remain paramount. Apart from the acknowledged masters whose works abound in the Louvre, many appealing artists, some only recently rediscovered, are scarcely represented if at all. The Louvre collection is undoubtedly without rival, and what needs to be done now is to give it the finishing touches and to represent the neo-classical period as completely as possible, showing all its many nuances.

<

Jean-Baptiste Regnault
Paris, 1754 – Paris, 1829
The Descent from the Cross
1789

Canvas
425 x 233 cm
*Commissioned for the chapel
in the Château de Fontainebleau*

∨

**Jean-François-Pierre
Peyron**
Aix-en-Provence, 1744 –
Paris, 1814
The funeral of Miltiades
1782

Canvas
98 x 136 cm
*Seized during the French
Revolution from the collection
of the Comte d'Angiviller*

∧
Jacques Louis David
Paris, 1748 – Brussels, 1825
The oath of the Horatii
1784

Canvas
330 x 425 cm
Collection of Louis XVI

Executed in Rome, this canvas was enthusiastically received when it was exhibited at the Paris Salon of 1785. Like Caravaggio's depictions of scenes from the life of St Matthew before, and Picasso's Demoiselles d'Avignon *after,* The oath of the Horatii *was to prove one of the great turning-points in the history of art. The sober realism, rigorous simplification of form and heroic tone of the subject-matter were all to be of significant influence on painting in the future.*

> **Jean-Germain Drouais**
Paris, 1763 – Rome, 1788
Marius at Minturnae
1786

Canvas
271 x 365 cm
Purchased in 1816

v
Jacques Louis David
Paris, 1748 – Brussels, 1825
The Sabine women
1799

Canvas
385 x 522 cm
Purchased in 1819

By judicious grouping of the figures and clear lighting, David has avoided the muddle and confusion that could have resulted from the depiction of such a huge crowd. The consecration took place in the Cathedral of Notre Dame, Paris, in the presence of Pope Pius VII. Although the painting contains many individual realistic portraits, it also achieves a general feeling of dignity and grandeur. David could well have based the composition on that of Rubens' The coronation of Marie de Médicis, *originally in the Palais du Luxembourg and now in the Louvre.*

Λ

Jacques Louis David
Paris, 1748 – Brussels, 1825
Portrait of the artist
1794

Canvas
81 x 64 cm
Presented by Eugène Isaberg, 1852

V

Jacques Louis David
Paris, 1748 – Brussels, 1825
Madame Trudaine
Circa 1792 (?)

Canvas
130 x 98 cm
*Bequeathed by Horace
Paul Delaroche, 1890*

> **Jacques Louis David**
Paris, 1748 –
Brussel, 1825
Madame Récamier
1800

Canvas
174 x 244 cm
Purchased in 1826

v
Jacques Louis David
Paris, 1748 –
Brussels, 1825
*The Consecration
of the Emperor
Napoleon and
Coronation of the
Empress Josephine,
2nd December 1804*
1806/7

Canvas
621 x 979 cm
*Commissioned
by Napoleon I*

<

Antoine Berjon
Lyons, 1754 – Lyons, 1843
*Still life with a basket
of flowers*
1814

Canvas
66 x 50 cm
Purchased in 1974

v

Louis Leopold Boilly
La Bassée, 1761 – Paris, 1845
*Meeting of artists
in Isabey's studio*
Exhibited at the Salon of 1798

Canvas
71.5 x 111 cm
*Bequeathed by Monsieur Biesta
Monrival, 1901*

>
**Pierre Henri
de Valenciennes**
Toulouse, 1750 –
Paris, 1819
*View of Rome
in the morning*
Circa 1782/84

Oil on paper laid on board
18 x 25 cm
*Collection of
Comte de l'Espine
Presented by Princesse
Louis de Croy, 1930*

∨
Joseph Bidauld
Carpentras, 1758 –
Montmorency, 1846
Landscape in Italy
1793

Canvas
113 x 144 cm
*Purchased at the
Salon of 1793*

<
Pierre-Paul Prud'hon
Cluny, 1758 – Paris, 1823
The Empress Josephine
1805

Canvas
244 x 179 cm
Collection of Napoleon III
Presented in 1879

∨
Pierre-Paul Prud'hon
Cluny, 1758 – Paris, 1823
Justice and Divine
Vengeance
pursuing Crime
1808

Canvas
244 x 294 cm
Commissioned for the Palais
de Justice, Paris, and exchanged
with the City of Paris in 1826

v
Pierre Paul Prud'hon
Cluny, 1758 – Paris, 1823
Venus bathing
Circa 1810

Canvas
134 x 103 cm
Purchased in 1932

^
François Gérard
Rome, 1770 – Paris, 1837
Cupid and Psyche
1798

Canvas
186 x 132 cm
Purchased in 1822

<
Pierre-Paul Prud'hon
Cluny, 1758 – Paris, 1823
*Portrait of the King
of Rome*
1811

Canvas
46 x 56 cm
Given in lieu of death duty, 1982

^
**Anne-Louis Girodet
de Roucy-Trioson**
Montargis, 1767 – Paris, 1824
The Sleep of Endymion
1793

Canvas
198 x 261 cm
Purchased in 1818

Atala, or the love of two savages in the desert, *was published by Chateaubriand in 1801 and inspired several painters. They were seduced by the exotic subject-matter – the story of the hopeless love of an Indian maiden, Atala, for a fellow Indian, Chactas, set in Louisiana in the eighteenth century. The tender and melancholy feeling in the painting and the importance given to the contrast of light and shade, diametrically opposed to David's style, is indicative of a 'pre-Romantic' sensibility, often one of the most attractive aspects of painting during the neo-classical period. In an even more dramatic and heightened manner, Prud'hon's moonlit* Justice and Divine Vengeance pursuing Crime *shows the same preoccupations, also very much 'anti-David'.*

>
**Anne-Louis Girodet
de Roucy-Trioson**
Montargis, 1767 – Paris 1824
*Portrait of the young
Romainville-Trioson*
1800

Canvas
73 x 59 cm
Purchased in 1991

∨
**Anne-Louis Girodet
de Roucy-Trioson**
Montargis, 1767 – Paris, 1824
The entombment of Atala
1808

Canvas
207 x 267 cm
Purchased in 1818

<
**Elisabeth Louise
Vigée-Lebrun**
Paris, 1755 – Paris, 1842
Hubert Robert, artist
1788

Wood
105 x 84 cm
*Presented by Madame
Tripier le Franc, 1843*

>
François Gérard
Rome, 1770 – Paris, 1837
*Jean-Baptiste Isabey,
miniaturist,
with his daughter*
1795

Canvas
194.5 x 130 cm
*Presented by Eugène Isabey,
1852*

>
Pierre-Narcisse Guérin
Paris, 1774 – Rome, 1833
Dido and Aeneas
1815 or just before

Canvas
35 x 45 cm
Bequeathed by Adrien-Aimé
Destouches, 1891

v
Pierre-Narcisse Guérin
Paris, 1774 – Rome, 1833
The return of Marcus Sextus
1799

Canvas
217 x 243 cm
Purchased in 1830

> Antoine-Jean
Gros
Paris, 1771 –
Meudon, 1835
Madame Pasteur
Circa 1795/96

Canvas
86 x 67 cm
*Presented by Charles
Pasteur, 1948*

<
Antoine-Jean Gros
Paris, 1771 –
Meudon, 1835
Christine Boyer
Circa 1800

Canvas
214 x 134 cm
Purchased in 1894

∨
Antoine-Jean-Gros
Paris, 1771 – Meudon, 1835
*Napoleon Bonaparte visiting
the plague-stricken at Jaffa, 1799*
1804

Canvas
523 x 715 cm
Commissionned by the State

This vast scene, full of warmth and lyricism, is a good example of the interest in the Orient instigated by Napoleon's battle campaigns. The subject-matter is actually little more than political propaganda, but its execution and the strong emotional appeal achieved by the simple treatment of the victims' fevered rapture, renders this canvas the first great success of Romanticism in painting.

∧
Antoine-Jean Gros
Paris, 1771 – Meudon, 1835
Napoleon Bonaparte on the battlefield of Eylau, 1807
1808

Canvas
521 x 784 cm
Commissioned after an open competition in 1807

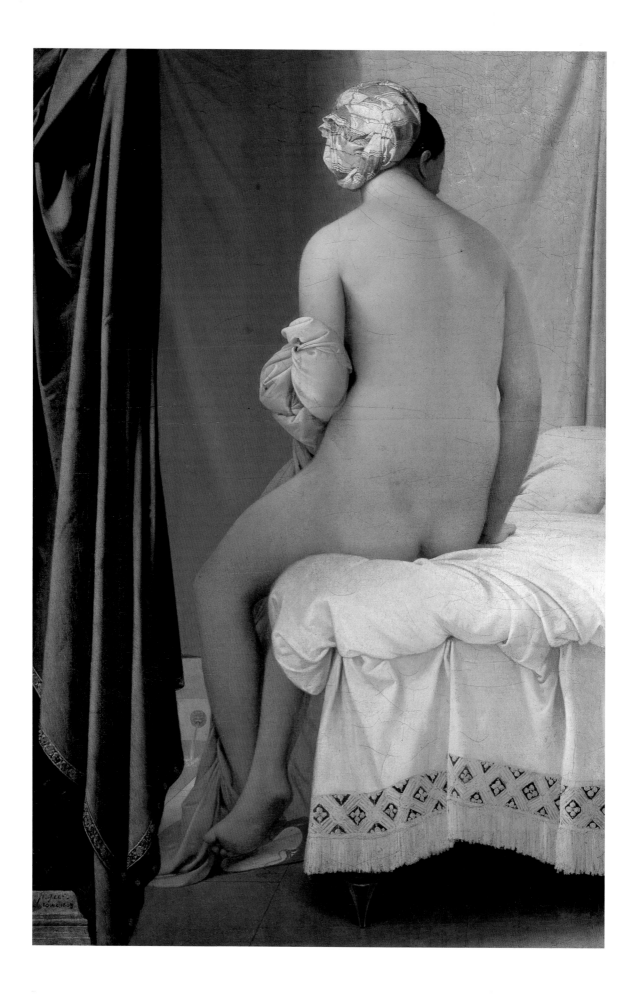

The nineteenth century

During the reigns of Louis XVIII and Charles X
the collection acquired several masterpieces by living
artists purchased directly from the Salon.

These included Ingres' *Roger and Angelica* **1819, Delacroix's** *Dante and Virgil* **and** *The massacre at Chios*, **in 1822 and 1824 respectively, and the huge canvases by Delaroche, Devéria and Scheffer in 1828.** The royal administration had a reputation for banal and conventional taste, but these acquisitions show that it was not necessarily always bad. In fact it could even be courageous, as in the famous purchase of the scandalous *The raft of the Medusa* by Géricault, the subject of which was a contemporary event exploited by the Opposition to fight the existing régime. The canvas, purchased by Dedreux-Dorcy at the artist's posthumous sale in 1824, was sold the following year to the Museum for its original price. All contemporary paintings were exhibited in the Musée du Luxembourg, which opened as the 'Galerie royale du Luxembourg' in 1818 exclusively for the works of living artists. They were not hung in the Louvre until later.

A major contribution to the Louvre during the Restoration in terms of contemporary art was not in the field of easel painting but in that of decoration. Ambitious designs for the Museum's new galleries have left the building with an impressive series of huge painted ceilings which are perhaps still not sufficiently studied. Of particular beauty are the two parallel series of rooms along the first floor of the south wing of the Cour Carrée, which today is still known as the Musée Charles X and houses the collections of Greek, Roman and Egyptian art. The ceilings of the Conseil d'État in the west wing of the Cour Carrée (now the Department of Objets d'Art) were also painted at this time, as were those rooms near the principal staircases of the Louvre (Salle Percier et Fontaine, and Salle Duchâtel). Thus many history painters, sometimes more conscientious than inspired, but in whom interest is now once again being revived, are represented permanently in the Louvre by their most ambitious works without the Museum having to purchase them or extract them from the reserve collections. Involved in this massive decorative scheme were not only ordinary artists such as Blondel, Picot, Alaux, M. M. Drolling and Mauzaisse, but also good painters such as Meynier, Heim, Schnetz, Abel de Pujol and Couder and true innovators such as E. Devéria, A.E. Fragonard (son of Jean-Honoré), L. Cogniet and H. Vernet grandson of Claude-Joseph). Neither should the last and possibly less accomplished works by the brilliant Baron Gros be forgotten, nor one of Ingres'most elaborate compositions, *The apotheosis of Homer.* This last-mentioned work was removed during the artist's lifetime and transformed into an easel painting for the Exposition Universelle of 1855 and was replaced by a copy painted by the Balze brothers.

<
**Jean Auguste
Dominique Ingres**
Montauban, 1780 –
Paris, 1867
The bather, known as
The Valpinçon bather
1908

Canvas
146 x 97 cm
Purchased in 1879

During Louis-Philippe's reign the most important scheme was the Musée historique in the Château de Versailles, and the major commissions during this period were always destined for Versailles. There the emphasis was not on the decoration of an existing museum, as Charles X had done with the Louvre, but the formation of an entire collection of exhibits at the same time, all with a pomp not seen since the time of Louis XIV. The Galerie des Batailles alone is a matter for wonder. In 1885 the Louvre acquired Delacroix's *The entry of the Crusaders into Constantinople* from the museum in Versailles and this unforgettable canvas, full of melancholy and passion, is a fitting echo of Veronese's and Rubens'great works hanging nearby.

The most beautiful Delacroix continued to be purchased at the Salon: *The women of Algiers* in 1834, and *The Jewish wedding* in 1841. His masterpiece, *Liberty guiding the people,* one of the most glorious paintings in the Louvre, had been purchased by Louis-Philippe in 1831. However, the influence of the painting's message was so feared by the Government that it was only exhibited for a few weeks in the Musée du Luxembourg. It was then returned to Delacroix and remained hidden except for a brief time in 1849. It was later shown at the Exposition Universelle of 1855, was exhibited at the Musée du Luxembourg again from 1861 and finally reached the Louvre in 1874. Paradoxically, Delacroix's great rival, Ingres, despite being a classical painter and ardent follower of Raphael, was much less well treated by the State, who bought few of his works; the scandalous and revolutionary Delacroix, prime exponent of Romantic art, fared much better. Ingres'portrait of *Cherubini* was purchased in 1842, and he was commissioned to paint *The Virgin with Eucharistic wafer,* which he did not complete until 1854. Louis-Philippe's major contribution to the Louvre's collection of works by Ingres was the fascinating series of twenty-five cartoons for the stained glass windows in the chapels of Saint-Ferdinand de Paris and Saint-Louis de Dreux executed between 1842 and 1844. Couture's *The Romans of the decadence,* commissioned by the State, was purchased in 1847.

The brief but generous Republic of 1848 purchased works by Géricault, five in 1849, and the vast, sublime images of *The officer of the Imperial Guard charging* and *The wounded officer of the Imperial Guard leaving the battlefield* at the sale of Louis-Philippe's possessions in 1851, as well as commissioning Duban to execute the restoration of the Galerie d'Apollon. The painted decoration was not completed and the central panel of the vaulted ceiling was painted by Delacroix between 1850 and 1851 with a scene depicting *Apollo vanquishing the Python*. Full of innovative lyricism, it is also magnificently in keeping with the paintings by Le Brun and eighteenth-century masters which surround it.

The acquisitions policy of the Second Empire was eclectic. Works by Delaunay, Baudry, Carolus-Duran, Gérôme, Lenepveu, Meissonier and other good academic artists, which are today exhibited in the Musée d'Orsay, were purchased. Also, more adventurously, two Corots were acquired, *The dance of the nymphs* in 1851 and the famous *Souvenir de Mortefontaine* at the Salon of 1864. Several works of Chassériau, Daubigny, Decamps and Rousseau were bought, and Gustave Moreau's *Orpheus* entered the Musée du Luxembourg in 1867. However, works of the great contemporary innovators of the Realist movement, who rejected official academic teaching, were not allowed into the Museum. Neither Millet, Courbet, Daumier, Troyon nor Dupré were exhibited.

Not until the end of the century and after the artists'deaths was the injustice rectified. Courbet's *The wave* was purchased in 1878 and several masterpieces including the *Wounded man* were purchased at the sale of the artist's studio in 1881. In the same year, Juliette Courbet gave *The burial at Ornans,* one of her brother's most important works which, along with the other Courbets has been in the Musée d'Orsay since 1986. The Millet canvases too are now on display there. Several of Millet's works were acquired at his posthumous sale in 1875; Madame Hartmann gave *Spring* in 1887 and Madame Pommery *The gleaners* in 1890. It was also after Ingres'death that several of his masterpieces came into the collection: among bequests were the three portraits of the Rivière family by Monsieur and Madame Rivière's daughter-in-law in 1870; *Oedipus* and *The spring* bequeathed by the Comtesse Duchâtel in 1878; and *Cordier* by Comtesse Mortier in 1886. Purchases included the portrait of *Monsieur Bochet* in 1878, the *Valpinçon bather* in 1879, the famous *Monsieur Bertin* and *The 'grande odalisque'* in 1899. The series was crowned by the Société des Amis du Louvre's gift of *The Turkish bath* in 1911.

Three large gifts in the early years of this century meant that big collections of small or medium-sized paintings entered the Louvre and ensured magnificent representation of artists such as Corot, Delacroix, Decamps, Millet and the Barbizon School of landscape painters. In 1902, Thomy Thiéry, and Englishman of French origin from Mauritius living in Paris, bequeathed a collection consisting entirely of nineteenth-century paintings, among them Delacroix's *Medea, The abduction of Rebecca,* nine small canvases and many splendid Corots and Barbizon paintings. This collection, which has remained together, is still on display at the Louvre following the opening of the Musée d'Orsay. Even richer and more varied was the collection given by Étienne Moreau-Nélaton in 1906. It comprised no less than thirty-seven superbly selected Corots and several master-pieces by Delacroix, including *Still life with a lobster* and *Young girl in the graveyard,* as well as a sketch by Géricault for *The raft of the Medusa.* The Moreau-Nélaton collection included the most avant-garde and truly innovative of contemporary art and it was through this collection that the Louvre acquired several Manet's, including the well-known *Déjeuner sur l'herbe,* a series of exquisite landscapes by Claude Monet and paintings by Berthe Morisot, Sisley and Pissarro. The whole collection was exhibited in the Musée des Arts Décoratifs for a long time and did not enter the Louvre until 1934. Its Impressionist paintings, after having been exhibited in the Musée du Jeu de Paume, are now housed in the Musée d'Orsay. The third gift (1909), which is today exhibited in its entirety in the Musée d'Orsay, was made by Alfred Chauchard in 1909, a fine collection of works by Corot, Delacroix, Millet, Diaz, Decamps, Dupré, Daubigny and Meissonier often acquired at high prices. The sum of 800,000 francs paid by Chauchard in 1889 for Millet's *Angelus* caused a sensation at the time. The Camondo bequest in 1911 also included fine Delacroixs and Corots, as well as splendid Impressionists.

After the First World War the Louvre made several spectacular acquisitions in the field of nineteenth-century art. Courbet's masterpiece, *The artist's studio,* which is today exhibited, along with the other Courbets, in the Musée d'Orsay, was purchased in 1920 with the help of both a public subscription and the Société des Amis du Louvre, and Delacroix's *The death of Sardanapalus,* one of the greatest expressions of Romantic art, was purchased the following year. The generosity of owners, descendants of great artists, keen to see their forebears'oeuvre well represented in the Louvre, or of private collectors, has continued to this day. In the first category, Baron Arthur Chassériau should be mentioned above all. His fine gift in 1918 and bequest in 1933/34 amounted to forty-three canvases by his uncle showing the whole range of that artist's genius.

Recently, private benefactors have been particularly generous. The portraits of *Bartolini* and *Madame Panckoucke* by Ingres, were presented by Carlos Beistegui in 1942 together with *The barricade* and another small work by Meissonier. In 1965 Baronne Gourgaud gave works by Corot and two splendid pieces by Delacroix and Daumier; James N.B. Hill gave in 1962 and bequeathed in 1978 a collection of works by Daubigny, Troyon, Corot and Millet and Courbet's portraits of *Pierre-Joseph Prud'hon* and *Madame Prud'hon* were presented by the sitter's grand-daughters in 1958. Two other beautiful Courbets, *The trout* and the *Nude figure with a dog* were recently received in lieu of death duties (1978 and 1979) and are now exhibited with the other Courbets in the Musée d'Orsay. The Beurdeley bequest in 1979 completed the dazzling collection of works by Delacroix with the landscape *The sea from the cliffs at Dieppe,* an extraordinary painting like a Claude Monet seen through the eyes of Titian.

As the vast sphere of nineteenth-century art still has many scantly-explored areas, it is difficult to form a clear idea of exactly what the Louvre should exhibit in order to give an accurate impression of the century and to emphasise its particular innovations. The Louvre, of course, favours the acknowledged masters, and is apt to mirror the taste of late nineteenth-century collectors. However, there is now room for greater variety in the collection and a more comprehensive coverage of the period, for yet again taste has changed.

The creation of the Musée d'Orsay, which is devoted to the art of the second half of the nineteenth century, has fundamentally altered the balance of the collections of nineteenth-century French painting in the Louvre. Courbet, Millet, Daumier, the landscape painters of the Barbizon school have crossed the Seine, along with Puvis de Chavannes, Moreau, Couture, Meissonier and the academic painters. Some canvases from the end of the careers of Ingres, Delacroix, Chassériau and Corot, essential to an appreciation of the painting of the Second Empire, have also been transferred to the Musée d'Orsay. However, the masterpieces of these artists, even their late works, have remained in the Louvre, so that their full careers can be traced: the *Turkish bath* by Ingres, the paintings of the Cour des Comptes by Chassériau, Corot's *Woman in blue* and *Bell tower of Douai.* Thus the bulk of the canvases from the first half of the nineteenth century can still be compared with the major works of earlier centuries. The opening of the Musée d'Orsay has provided an opportunity to cast a fresh eye over the painting of the second quarter of the nineteenth century, and to enrich the Museum's collections of this period; this policy has already led to the acquisition of canvases by Chassériau, Flandrin, Dubufe, Alexandre-Evariste Fragonard and Hesse.

>
**Jean Auguste
Dominique Ingres**
Montauban, 1780 –
Paris, 1867
Mademoiselle Rivière
Exhibited at the Salon of 1806

Canvas
100 x 70 cm
*Bequeathed by Madame Rivière,
1870*

∨
**Jean Auguste
Dominique Ingres**
Montauban, 1780 – Paris, 1867
The 'grand odalisque'
1814

Canvas
91 x 162 cm
Purchased in 1899

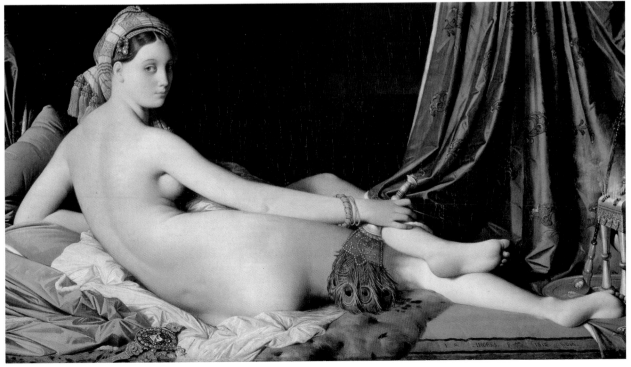

<
**Jean Auguste
Dominique Ingres**
Montauban, 1780 –
Paris, 1867
The sword of Henry IV
1832

Canvas
32 x 28 cm
*Purchased with the assistance
of the Société des Amis
du Louvre, 1981*

∨
**Jean Auguste
Dominique Ingres**
Montauban, 1780 –
Paris, 1867
The apotheosis of Homer
1827

Canvas
386 x 512 cm
*Originally a ceiling painting
in the Salle Clarac in the Louvre,
commissioned in 1826*

The female nude was a subject that interested Ingres all his life. The Turkish bath, *the last of his many variations on the theme, shows, as does* The 'grande odalisque', *the fascination exerted by the Orient throughout the nineteenth-century. The* Valpinçon Bather *is a youthful work, painted hilst Ingres was staying at the Villa Medici. He was subsequently to return several times to this motif of a nude seen from behind, most notably fifty-four years later in* The Turkish bath.

∧
Jean Auguste Dominique Ingres
Montauban, 1780 – Paris, 1867
The Turkish bath
1862

Canvas on wood
Diameter 108 cm
Presented by the Société des Amis du Louvre, 1911

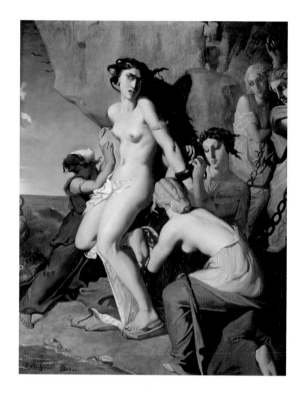

∨
Théodore Chassériau
Sainte-Barbe de Samana,
1819 – Paris, 1856
*Andromeda and
the Nereids*
1840

Canvas
92 x 74 cm
Purchased in 1986

∧
**Jean Auguste
Dominique Ingres**
Montauban, 1780 –
Paris, 1867
Monsieur Bertin
1832

Canvas
116 x 95 cm
Purchased in 1897

>
Marius Granet
Aix-en-Provence,
1755 –
Aix-en-Provence,
1849
*S Trinità dei Monti
and the Villa
Média, Rome*
1808

Canvas
48 x 61 cm
Anonymous gift, 1981

^
Théodore Chassériau
Sainte-Barbe-de-Samana,
1819 – Paris, 1856
The toilet of Esther
1841

Canvas
45.5 x 35.5 cm
*Bequeathed by Baron Arthur
Chassériau, 1934*

^
Théodore Chassériau
Sainte-Barbe-de-Samana,
1819 – Paris, 1856
*The two sisters
(the artist's sisters)*
1843

Canvas
180 x 135 cm
*Bequeathed by Baron and
Baronne Arthur Chassériau, 1918*

Théodore Chassériau
Sainte-Barbe-de-Samana,
1819 – Paris, 1856
Peace
Between 1844 and 1848

Canvas
340 x 362 cm
*Fragment from the decoration
of the building of the Cour des
Comptes, burnt in 1871
Bequeathed by the Chassériau
Committee, 1903*

<
Théodore Géricault
Rouen, 1781 – Paris, 1824
*The wounded officer
of the Imperial Guard
leaving the battlefield*
Exhibited at the Salon
of 1814

Canvas
358 x 294 cm
Purchased in 1851

*This painting was a 'succès de scandale' at the Salon of 1819, recalling
the wreck of the* Medusa *in 1816 and the shameful inability of the captain
to save his passengers, except a few who were crowded together on a raft.
After a long time at sea, further deaths and even instances of cannibalism,
the survivors were finally rescued. Géricault made several studies of dying
people and corpses in hospitals before executing this sublime painting –
one of the greatest visual interpretations of human suffering.*

V
Théodore Géricault
Rouen, 1781 – Paris, 1824
The raft of the Medusa
Exhibited at the Salon of 1819

Canvas
491 x 716 cm
Purchased in 1824

∧
Théodore Géricault
Rouen, 1781 – Paris, 1824
The madwoman
Circa 1822

Canvas
77 x 64.5 cm
Presented by the Société
des Amis du Louvre, 1938

>
Théodore Géricault
Rouen, 1781 – Paris, 1824
The plaster kiln
Circa 1822/23

Canvas
50 x 61 cm
Purchased in 1849

∧
Théodore Géricault
Rouen, 1781 – Paris, 1824
The Epsom Derby
1821

Canvas
92 x 122 cm
Purchased in 1866

Painted in 1821, during Géricault's stay in London, the canvas takes its inspiration from English sporting prints, which frequently depict horses at the 'flying gallop' shown by the painter here. The invention of photography, by allowing the various movements of a galloping animal to be analysed, would allow it to be painted accurately, as Degas was to do in his Race-course *paintings.*

*A spectacular illustration of the enthusiasm aroused amongst the romantic youth by
the revolt of the Greeks against the Turks,* The massacre at Chios *was directly inspired
by the savage Turkish repression of the population of the island of Chios in April 1822.
The critics at the Salon of 1824 received this fine painting very unfavourably. Delacroix
had been inspired by Constable's* Haywain, *which was exhibited at the same Salon,
reworking the landscape background with a vibrant touch.*

^
Eugène Delacroix
Charenton-Saint-Maurice,
1798 – Paris, 1863
The massacre at Chios
1824

Canvas
419 x 354 cm
Purchased at the Salon of 1824

>
Eugene Delacroix
Charenton-Saint-Maurice,
1798 – Paris, 1863
*Liberty guiding the people,
28th July 1830*
1830

Canvas
260 x 325 cm
Purchased at the Salon of 1831

v
Eugène Delacroix
Charenton-Saint-Maurice,
1798 – Paris, 1863
The death of Sardanapalus
Exhibited at the Salon
of 1827/28

Canvas
392 x 496 cm
Purchased in 1921

<

Eugène Delacroix
Charenton-Saint-Maurice,
1798 – Paris, 1863
*The sea from the cliffs
at Dieppe*
1852 (?)

Cardboard on wood
35 x 51 cm
*Bequeathed by Marcel Beurdeley,
1979*

v

Eugène Delacroix
Charenton-Saint-Maurice,
1798 – Paris, 1863
The women of Algiers
1834

Canvas
180 x 229 cm
Purchased at the Salon of 1834

One of Delacroix's lesser-known masterpieces, the subject-matter was dictated by its destination. Appollo vanquishing the Python *shows the painter working in a direct line from the great decorators of the seventeenth and eighteenth centuries, without losing any of his own ardour or lyricism.*

Λ
Eugène Delacroix
Charenton-Saint-Maurice,
1798 – Paris, 1863
*Apollo vanquishing
the Python*
1850/51

Mural painting
About 800 x 750 cm
*Central panel of the vaulted
ceiling of the Galerie d'Apollon
in the Louvre*

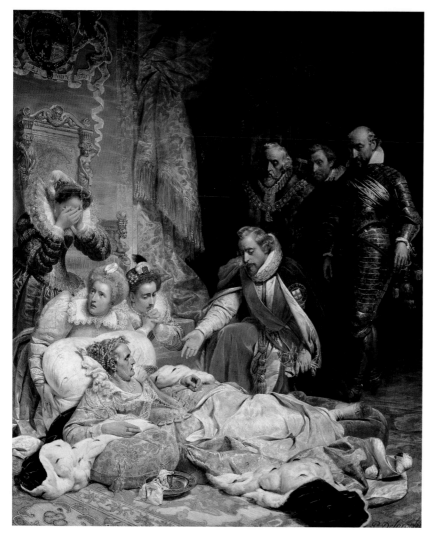

<
Ary Scheffer
Dordrecht, 1795 – Argenteuil, 1858
*The ghosts of Paolo and Francesca
appear to Dante and Virgil*
1855 (copy by the artist of a painting
first executed in 1822)

Canvas
171 x 239 cm
*Bequeathed by Madame
Marjolin-Scheffer, 1900*

∧
Hippolyte Flandrin
Lyon, 1809 – Paris, 1864
Young man by the sea
1837

Canvas
98 x 124 cm
*Entered the Musée de
Luxembourg in 1857*

<
Paul Delaroche
Paris, 1797 – Paris, 1856
*The death of Elizabeth I,
Queen of England*
1828

Canvas
422 x 343 cm
*Purchased at the Salon
of 1827/28*

>
Horace Vernet
Paris, 1789 – Paris, 1863
The gate at Clichy
1820

*Entered the Musée du
Luxembourg in 1837*

v
Léopold Robert
La Chaux-de-Fonds, 1794 –
Venice, 1835
*The Pilgrimage to the
Madonna of the Arch*
1827

Canvas
142 x 212 cm
Purchased at the Salon of 1828

>
Octave Tassaert
Paris, 1800 – Paris, 1874
Studio interior
1845

Canvas
46 x 38 cm
Presented by Ernest May, 1923

v
Eugène Isabey
Paris, 1803 –
Montévrain, 1886
Beach at low tide
1833

Canvas
124 x 168 cm
Purchased at the Salon of 1833

∧
Hippolyte Flandrin
Lyons, 1809 – Paris, 1864
*Portrait of
Madame Flandrin*
1846

Canvas
83 x 66 cm
*Presented by Madame Foidevaux,
1984*

<
Paul Delaroche
Paris, 1797 – Paris, 1856
*Bonaparte crossing
the Alps*
1848

Canvas
289 x 222 cm
*Presented by M and
Mme Birkhauser, 1982*

<
Antoine-Louis Barye
Paris, 1795 – Paris, 1875
Lions near their den
Circa 1860

Canvas
38 x 49 cm
Thomy Thiéry bequest, 1902

v
**Alexandre Gabriel
Decamps**
Paris, 1803 –
Fontainebleau, 1860
The defeat of the Cimbri
1833

Canvas
130 x 195 cm
Bequeathed by Maurice Cottier, 1884

>
**Charles-François
Daubigny**
Paris, 1817 – Paris, 1878
The floodgate at Optevoz
1859

Canvas
48,5 x 73 cm
*Bequeathed by Thomy Thiéry,
1902*

<
**Alexandre Gabriel
Decamps**
Paris, 1803 –
Fontainebleau, 1860
The monkey painter
1833

Canvas
32 x 40 cm
Thomy Thiéry bequest, 1902

v
Théodore Rousseau
Paris, 1812 – Barbizon, 1867
*Group of oak trees,
Apremont*
1852

Canvas
63,5 x 99,5 cm
*Bequeathed by Thomy Thiéry,
1902*

<
Théodore Rousseau
Paris, 1812 –
Barbizon, 1867
Spring
Circa 1852

Canvas
41 x 63 cm
*Thomy Thiéry
bequest, 1902*

v
Constant Troyon
Sèvres, 1810 –
Paris, 1865
*View from the heights
of Suresnes*
1856

Canvas
182 x 265 cm
*Thomy Thiéry
bequest, 1902*

Corot's work is represented in the Louvre by almost 150 paintings – more than in any other museum. He brought a matchless emotive note to landscape painting in his accurate evocation of the golden light of Italy or the softer light of the Île-de France and the Beauce.

>
**Jean-Baptiste
Camille Corot**
Paris, 1796 – Paris, 1875
Chartres Cathedral, 1830
Retouched in 1872

Canvas
64 x 51.5 cm
*Bequeathed by Étienne
Moreau-Nélaton, 1906*

v
**Jean-Baptiste
Camille Corot**
Paris, 1796 – Paris, 1875
Volterra
1834

Canvas
70.5 x 94 cm
*Bequeathed by Étienne
Moreau-Nélaton, 1906*

>
**Jean-Baptiste
Camille Corot**
Paris, 1796 – Paris, 1875
*Portrait of Marie-Laure
Sennegon*
1831

Canvas
28 x 21 cm
*Bequeathed by Corot
Presented by Etienne
Moreau-Nélaton, 1921*

v
**Jean-Baptiste
Camille Corot**
Paris, 1796 – Paris, 1875
The Bridge at Narmi
1826

Paper on canvas
34 x 48 cm
*Bequeathed by Etienne
Moreau-Nélaton, 1921*

>
**Jean-Baptiste
Camille Corot**
Paris, 1769 – Paris, 1875
Woman with a Pearl
Circa 1869

Canvas
70 x 55 cm
Purchased in 1902

∨
**Jean-Baptiste
Camille Corot**
Paris, 1796 – Paris, 1875
Souvenir de Mortefontaine
Exhibited at the Salon
of 1864

Canvas
65 x 89 cm
Purchased at the Salon of 1864

> Jean-Baptiste
Camille Corot
Paris, 1796 – Paris, 1875
*The interior
of Sens cathedral*
1874

Canvas
61 x 40 cm
Gift of Jacques Zoubaloff, 1919

< Jean-Baptiste
Camille Corot
Paris, 1796 – Paris, 1875
Woman in blue
1874

Canvas
80 x 50.5 cm
Purchased in 1912

*The female figures executed by Corot entirely for his own enjoyment, particularly at the end
of his life, are now often admired as much, if not more, than the landscapes for which he is
traditionally famous. One of the last and perhaps the most beautiful of these female studies,
unknown to the public during Corot's lifetime, is the* Woman in blue, *a triumph in the
handling of paint and a fine example of strength of composition and grandiose simplicity.*

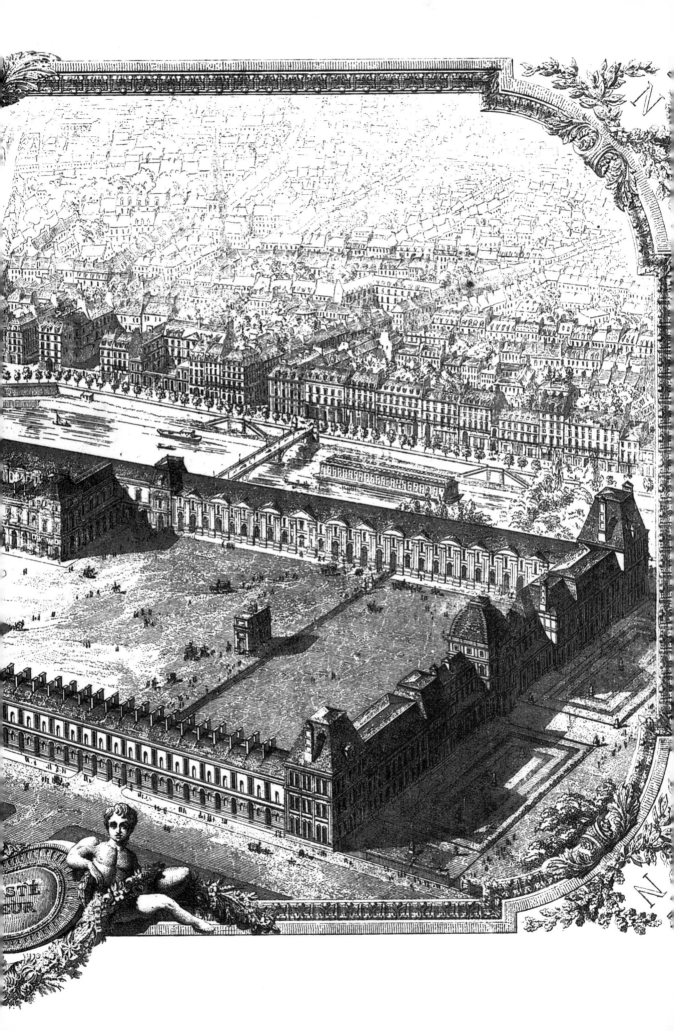

European painting

Michel Laclotte

The Salon Carré, at the eastern end of the Grande Galerie, is one of the most famous rooms in the Louvre. The official exhibitions of contemporary French paintings mounted by the Académie Royale de Peinture et de Sculpture were held here from their inception at the beginning of the eighteenth century until the mid-nineteenth century. It was this tradition that gave rise to the name 'Salon' for temporary exhibitions of paintings. Castiglione's painting shows the room just after 1851 when it had been redecorated and given a sumptuous new ceiling by Duban and Simart. The Salons now took place elsewhere and the dense display of paintings in this picture comprises a selection of the most renowned masterpieces in the Louvre at the time–all schools of painting and periods mixed together. Today the Salon Carré is devoted entirely to French fifteenth- and sixteenth-century art.

<

Giuseppe Castiglione
*View of the Salon Carré
in 1861*
1861

Introduction

Cézanne once said 'It seems to me that the Louvre has all we need, that everything can be loved and understood there'. Few of the great museums of the world contain such varied collections of all schools of European painting from the end of the thirteenth to the nineteenth century, and illustrate such diverse styles and formats. The collections range from small, intimate paintings to monumental canvases, from frescoes to whole decorative schemes, and offer examples of schools rarely represented outside their native countries. The wide range of the collection, despite the inevitable serious gaps and weaker sections, is the result of the long history of the formation of the collection over more than four and a half centuries and of the fact that it was a royal collection before it became a national museum. The nineteenth- and twentieth-century acquisitions followed the evolution of taste and the discovery of the discipline of art history, and the royal collection was thus complemented and balanced by previously unknown or disregarded paintings.

It is often forgotten that the collection originated in the sixteenth century with a 'museum of modern art'. François I followed the example of his predecessor Louis XII, and with a bravado which was the envy of other European monarchs approached the most prestigious living artists, either buying their paintings or bringing them from Italy to work for him. The patronage of contemporary artists continued to sustain the royal collection, and the then 'Old Masters' were also purchased.

Not only does François I's collection of contemporary Italian paintings, given place of honour at the Château de Fontainebleau, testify to the personal taste of an enlightened prince, but it is also one of the clearest indications of the introduction from Italy into France of the Renaissance. François I called upon several French and Flemish painters (Jean Clouet and Joos van Cleve, for example), as Henri II and Catherine de Médicis were to do with François Clouet, but it would seem that this was solely for portraiture, a field in which the competence of Northern artists was acknowledged. It did not, nevertheless, prevent the King from asking Titian to paint his portrait.

After the reign of Henri IV, who used French artists or artists working in France, such as Ambroise Dubois, for the decoration of his residences, a short but brilliant period of royal patronage was initiated by Marie de Médicis. She commissioned Rubens to decorate the gallery of the Palais du Luxembourg in 1625 and she also employed another Flemish artist, Pourbus, and the Italian, Gentileschi, at a time when the most promising young French painters such as Vouet, Poussin, and Claude Lorrain were themselves in Italy and as yet unrecognised.

The great tradition of François I was resumed by Louis XIV. As soon as he took power in 1661, the King began to enrich the royal collection, advised by his minister Colbert, until its magnificence soon reflected that of the reign of the Sun King himself. This was largely thanks to two spectacular acquisitions: a large part of Cardinal Mazarin's famous collection, and in 1662 and 1671 that of the banker Everhard Jabach. Masterpieces of the Italian Renaissance which had always been revered (works by Leonardo, Raphael, and Titian and also by Correggio and Veronese), most of which had come from the collection of Charles I of England, were reunited with those from François I's collection, while the work of more recent artists such as Caravaggio and Guido Reni also entered the royal collection. It was continually enriched with other sixteenth-century paintings, particularly by the great Venetian artists, and by paintings from seventeenth-century Rome and Bologna which appealed to the French taste for classicism; a taste nurtured by the art of Poussin, Claude, Le Brun, and their followers. The northern Renaissance is also well represented in the collection of Louis XIV with an impressive series of portraits by Holbein and works by Beham and Antonio Moro. The acquisition of Dutch and Flemish art of the seventeenth century indicates the change in taste of both collectors and young artists themselves at the end of the century. More colourful and sensual painting, which exhibits not so much idealisation but rather expressive animation and, indeed, the picturesque, is exemplified by the paintings of Rembrandt, Rubens, and van Dyck.

Although magnificent private collections, which were to be gold mines for the princely galleries of Germany, for Catherine the Great, and for British collectors, were assembled under Louis XV, and although Paris became one of the centres of European art, the Cabinet du Roi (King's collection) hardly increased at all. Some foreign paintings, mostly bought from the estate of the Prince de Carignan in 1742, were added, and constituted an excellent selection, dominated by Flemish and Dutch art.

Towards the middle of the eighteenth century the public began to demand that the royal collections should be on general view. The idea of installing a suitable museum in the old palace of the Louvre materialised under Louis XVI. The Surintendant des Bâtiments, the Comte d'Angiviller, began a programme of acquisitions. His policy was not just a case of enriching the King's gallery with costly works in order to boost royal prestige; it was a deliberate effort to build up a more representative collection of the different schools of painting as they were known and appreciated at the time. The Age of Reason and of Diderot's 'Encyclopedia' demanded this approach. Additions to the foreign collection were principally to the Flemish and especially to the Dutch seventeenth-century sections. The Italian 'primitives' were still not appreciated, but there was another innovation in the acquisition of Spanish painting, at last represented in the royal collection by Murillo.

The project was completed by the French Revolution. The 'Muséum Central des Arts' was opened in the Louvre in 1793. The resources of the royal collection, now the national collection, were soon augmented by numerous paintings seized from churches or collectors who had emigrated and then, in the wake of French military victories, by masterpieces seized in Flanders and Holland, Italy and Germany. It was thus that a fabulous musuem, called the Musée Napoléon from 1803, was founded. It was dominated by foreign art: masters of the Renaissance and seventeenth century in Italy, Flanders, and Holland, but also early Flemish and early Italian masters and painters of the German Renaissance, rescued at last from oblivion. Today's international moral code would condemn such an enterprise, yet it would be wrong to attribute it simply to the ritual plundering of victorious armies. The Musée Napoléon was undoubtedly formed in the spirit of its creators, above all of its admirable director, Vivant Denon, as a High Temple of Art for the edification of the citizens of Imperial Europe. It was designed to illustrate the moral and intellectual progress which stemmed from the Revolution: in the words of Denon, the 'comparison of the efforts of the human spirit throughout the centuries'. The creation of other museums in the main provincial towns (such as Brussels, Geneva, Mainz, and Milan) with Parisian funds conformed to the same nobly educative policy.

In 1815, after Waterloo, representatives sent by the beleaguered countries took back more than five thousand works of art. Only about a hundred paintings escaped restitution and were left in the Louvre by the allies of France. However, the wealth of its reserves ensured the survival of the Museum. During the Restoration and the July Monarchy efforts were either directed elsewhere, to the creation under Louis XVIII of the Musée du Luxembourg for living artists, and, under Louis-Philippe, of the Musée de l'histoire de France at Versailles, or were without lasting benefit for the national heritage, as in the establishment of Louis-Philippe's Spanish collection, returned to the Orleans family after 1848 and shortly afterwards sold in England. But after the Revolution of 1848 and under the Second Empire, the Museum took on a new lease of life. Thereafter, and until the First World War, the curators were to be in competition with their English and German colleagues, and later American collectors, for the purchase of paintings missing in the collection. The history of art, now an acknowledged academic discipline, had begun to define the true perspectives of European painting, from early masters to the eighteenth century, resurrecting this or that artist or entire school from years of neglect. The continual purchases of collectors increased the rarity of works on the market, but the Louvre gradually filled some of the gaps in its collection, especially in the field of 'primitives'. The purchase of the Campana collection in 1863 consisted of about a hundred such 'primitive' Italian panels of the fourteenth and fifteenth centuries. The Spanish and English collections were also increased and Italian eighteenth-century paintings were bought. Simultaneously, the great variety in taste of the connoisseurs who generously gave or bequeathed works to the Louvre balanced and diversified the representation of different schools, whether recently brought to light or traditionally appreciated. In the first rank of these connoisseurs must be placed Dr La Caze, whose collection entered the Louvre in 1869.

Throughout the nineteenth century the abundance of French painting and its influence internationally on both official and avante-garde art distracted museum curators and French collectors alike from the contemporary art of other countries.

It was only from the end of the century that works representative of most of the European countries and of the United States were acquired for the Musée du Luxembourg (later these paintings were to form a special museum for modern foreign schools at the Musée du Jeu de Paume). This contemporary harvest was rich but uneven. Whistler's *The artist's mother,* and remarkable paintings by Winslow Homer, Watts, and Pelizza da Volpedo were acquired to the exclusion of Klimt or Munch, the most original of the Symbolists. All these paintings are now exhibited in the Musée d'Orsay with the French paintings of the same period from the national collections presented successively to the Jeu de Paume, the Louvre and the Palais de Tokyo.

Less stringent credit terms and new legal provisions which authorised gifts of works of art in lieu of death duties secured for the Louvre major works by Filippino Lippi, Rubens, Vermeer, Hals and Goya and have enabled the museum to pursue a new programme of acquisitions.

After 1918 the era of great purchases seems to be over. The Louvre bought Dürer's *Self portrait,* but lack of funds, despite the constant help and foresight of the Société des Amis du Louvre, prevented the possibility of acquiring masterpieces from private collections which foreign museums and art lovers, especially Americans, were able to acquire. Yet on the eve of the Second World War the spirit of the Museum was revived once again. A general reorganisation, which continued after the War, was begun. Several important donations from great and established collections (Rothschild, Groult, Péreire) or more recent ones (Beistegui, Nicolas, Lyon, Salavin) enriched different sections of the foreign schools. Less stringent credit terms and new legal provisions, which authorised the gift of works of art in lieu of death duties and thus secured for the Louvre major works by Filippino Lippi, Rubens, and Goya, enabled the pursuit of a new programme of acquisitions.

The redevelopment of the former Ministry of Finance, now the museum's Richelieu wing in the north of the palace, has allowed the department of paintings to expand considerably. The whole first floor of the south wing is devoted to the Italian school, the second floor of the Cour Carrée is given to the French school, with the large-scale works of the nineteenth century remaining in their vast rooms. Much of the remaining part of the second floor of the Richelieu wing is shared by the Flemish, Dutch, German and English schools.

The fourteenth and fifteenth centuries in Italy

From the sixteenth century, the early Italian masters
or 'primitives' had been neglected in favour of the classicism
of the High Renaissance.

Artist earlier than Perugino or Leonardo were absent from the French royal collections and from those of other European princes. The resurrection of the Trecento and Quattrocento artists began with the establishment of the Musée Napoléon at the beginning of the nineteenth century. Certain French art historians like Seroux d'Agincourt, or connoisseurs such as Artaud de Montor and Cacault, were amongst the pioneers of a rediscovery which was to earn the admiration of the Nazarenes in Germany and the exponents of the 'style troubadour' in France. This admiration did not become general before about 1825, although works by Mantegna and Giovanni Bellini had been included in the first convoys of paintings brought back from Italy in 1798 by the triumphant Napoleonic armies. The importance of the primitive Italian school of the remote Middle Ages was sensed by Vivant Denon, who was always anxious to broaden the horizons of his Museum. He went to Italy in 1811 to choose a series of fifteenth-century Florentine altarpieces by Fra Angelico, Filippo Lippi, Ghirlandaio, Lorenzo di Credi, and even older works, notably the altarpieces by Cimabue and Giotto from the church of San Francesco in Pisa. In Genoa he bought the triptych now attributed to Carlo Braccesco. When in 1815 the allies organised a large scale operation to return works of art to their countries of origin, this section of the Museum was less disrupted than most.

The following period of the Restoration and the July Monarchy was notoriously unprofitable for old collections. However, several isolated purchases deserve mention; the panels by the Master of the Codex of St George and the Master of Ovile from the collection of the troubadour painter Pierre-Henri Révoil; the *Birth of St John* by Signorelli in 1824; and, above all, the *Carrying of the Cross* by Simone Martini in 1834. This, like the other small panels from the same polyptych (now in the Fine Arts Museum, Antwerp), was acquired in Dijon and came from the Carthusian monastery of Champmol. The price of this exquisite masterpiece indicates the low regard in which the primitives were held at this time by all but a few isolated connoisseurs. The work was bought for the modest sum of 200 francs, while there was no hesitation in paying 250,000 francs for the *Nativity* by Spagna, a second-rate Umbrian painter whose work was overshadowed by that of Perugino and Raphael.

Under the Second Empire, the affair of the Campana collection caused a scandal which was to have important consequences for the Louvre. The Marquis Campana (1807-80),

<
Domenico Bigordi
called **Ghirlandaio**
Florence, 1449 –
Florence, 1494
*Portrait of an
old man and
a young boy*
Circa 1488

Wood
63 x 46 cm
Purchased in 1886

director of an important banking concern in Rome, had accumulated a fantastic collection of antiques and paintings by early masters in his palaces. Driven by his passion for collecting, he had begun to borrow increasingly large sums of money from the company which he directed, 'investing' them in his own collection. In 1857 the accounts were checked and the deficit revealed. Campana was arrested and sentenced to banishment and his collections were put up for sale. After secret negotiations and stiff competition between several great European museums, the collection of some 11,835 objects, including 646 paintings, was bought by Napoleon III for the vast sum of 4,360,400 francs. At first exhibited in its entirety at the Palais de l'Industrie from (1862), this unique collection was then brutally divided (in 1863, 1872, and 1876) between various provincial museums, the Louvre retaining only about a hundred Trecento and Quattrocento paintings. This senseless dispersal, decried in vain at the time by many artists, including Ingres and Delacroix, has now been remedied by regrouping the 300 primitives which had been scattered among local museums at the Petit Palais in Avignon, opened in 1976. The Campana collection in the Louvre is very varied, with special emphasis on the Tuscan School and on the Venetian and other northern Schools. Other centres of art, less appreciated and judged provincial at the time of the dispersal of the collection, are better represented at Avignon, and range from the Giottesque Florentine painters such as Bernardo Daddi to Bartolomeo Vivarini and Mantegna. Among the masterpieces from the collection in the Louvre are Uccello's *Battle,* Cosimo Tura's *Pietà,* and the series of *Famous men* from the Palazzo Ducale at Urbino by Justus of Ghent and Pedro Berruguete.

When these paintings entered the Louvre, the battle for the Italian primitives had been won. The fourteenth and fifteenth centuries, better known thanks to the research of the art historians Crowe and Cavalcaselle and later of Berenson, were worshipped by the English Pre-Raphaelites and their followers, and became henceforth the object of a universal craze. The keepers of the Louvre devoted themselves to the completion of the collections. Without managing to create a panorama as complete as their colleagues at the National Gallery in London, they nevertheless acquired distinguished works by Antonello da Messina, Baldovinetti, Jacopo and Giovanni Bellini, Pisanello, and Ghirlandaio, and also successfully acquired the allegorical frescoes by Fra Angelico from the convent of San Domenico in Fiesole. In 1910 the town of Aigueperse sold to the Louvre Mantegna's *St Sebastian,* which had belonged to the Gonzaga-Montpensier family.

It was not until the last 35 years, when the American collections' initial enthusiasm for buying Italian primitives had passed, that there were other noteworthy acquisitions in this area by the Louvre. Among these were the three great panels of the Borgo San Sepolcro reredos by Sassetta, bought in 1956 and joined fortuitously in 1965 and 1988 by two of the pictures from the predella of the same polyptych, and the *Calvary* by Giovanni Bellini (1970). Mention should also be made of the *Story of Esther* by Filippino Lippi, given in lieu of death duties in 1972 and which was originally the companion piece to another 'cassone' now at Chantilly; the strikingly monumental portrait of *Sigismondo Malatesta* by Piero della Francesca, one of the great masters whose absence from the Louvre had long been deplored (1978); Zoppo's *Madonna;* a precious thirteenth-century *Crucifixion* (Master of San Francesco) and several fourteenth-century Siennese pieces (Pietro Lorenzetti, Lippo Memmi, Ugolino) and, finally, the *Christ at the column* by Antonello da Messina which joined his *Condottiere* in 1992.

> **Cenni di Pepe,**
> *called* **Cimabue**
> Florence, circa 1240 –
> Florence, after 1302
> *Maesta; the Madonna*
> *and Child in Majesty*
> *surrounded by angels*
> Circa 1270 (?)
>
> Wood
> 427 x 280 cm
> *From the Church of*
> *San Francesco, Pisa*
> *Entered in 1814*

<
Giotto di Bondone
Colle di Vespignano,
circa 1267 – Florence, 1337
*St Francis of Assist
receiving the Stigmata*

Predella:
*The Vision of Pope
Innocent III; the Pope
receiving the statutes
of the Order; St Francis
preaching to the birds*
Circa 1295/1300 (?)

Wood
313 x 163 cm
*From the Church
of San Francesco, Pisa
Entered in 1814*

*Here Giotto revives some of the
compositions illustrating different
episodes of the life of St Francis as he
had painted them in the mural
frescoes of the Basilica at Assisi
during the last decade of the
thirteenth century. The four scenes
form a kind of abridged version of
the artist's original creation. Giotto's
main innovation was his ability to
represent holy figures as human
beings and as solid forms arranged
in three-dimensional space.*

<
Master of San Francesco
Active in Umbria, second half
of the thirteenth century
Painted cross
Circa 1260

Wood
86 x 73 cm
Purchased in 1981

v
Simone Martini
Siena, circa 1284 –
Avignon, 1344
The Carrying of the Cross
Circa 1336/42 (?)

Wood
28 x 16 cm
Purchased in 1834

∧
Pietro da Rimini
Active in Rimini
during the first half
of the 14th century
*The Deposition
from the Cross*
Circa 1330/40

Wood
43 x 35 cm
Brauer gift, 1932

>
Pietro Lorenzetti
Siena, documented
from 1305 (?) to 1345
*The Adoration
of the Magi*
Circa 1340

Wood
33 x 24 cm
Purchased in 1986

∧
**Master of the
St George Codex**
Active in Tuscany and
at Avignon (?) at the
beginning of the 14th century
*The Virgin and Child
on a throne surrounded
by angels; St John
the Baptist, St Peter,
and two saints*
Between 1320 and 1340

Wood
56 x 21 cm
Purchased in 1828

^

Bolognese painter
Triptych
1333

Central panel:
The Coronation of the Virgin,
The Crucifixion
Wood
73 x 135 cm

Left wing:
The Angel of the Annunciation,
The Madonna of Mercy,
Saints Margaret, Catherine,
and Lucy (?)

Right wing:
The Virgin of the Annunciation,
The Nativity, Three Martyr
Saints
Wood
127 x 36 cm (each wing)
Collection of the Marquis Campana
Purchased in 1863

Lorenzo Veneziano
Active in Venice from 1356 to 1372
The Madonna and Child
1372

Wood
126 x 56 cm
Collection of the Marquis Campana
Purchased in 1863

<
Giovanni di Milano
Active in Florence
between 1320 and 1369
St Francis of Assisi
Circa 1360

Wood
113 x 39 cm
Collection of the
Marquis Campana
Purchased in 1863

>
Antonio Pisano, *called* **Pisanello**
Verona (?) before 1395-? 1455 (?)
Portrait assumed to be of Ginevra d'Este
Circa 1436-8 (?)

Wood
43 x 30 cm
Purchased in 1893

v
Jacopo Bellini
Active in Venice from 1423 – Venice, 1470
*The Madonna and Child adored by
Lionello d'Este*
Circa 1450

Wood
60 x 40 cm
Purchased in 1873

v
Gentile da Fabriano
Fabriano, circa 1370 – Rome, 1427
The Presentation in the Temple
1423

Wood
26 x 66 cm
*From the church of Santa Trinita, Florence
Entered in 1814*

<
Fra Angelico
Vicchio di Mugello (?),
circa 1400 (?) – Rome, 1455
*The Martyrdom of St Cosmo
and St Damian*
Circa 1440

Wood
37 x 46 cm
Purchased circa 1882

∨
Filippo Lippi
Florence, circa 1406/07 –
Spoleto, 1469
*The Madonna and
Child surrounded by
Angels, with St Frediano
and St Augustine*
Circa 1437/8

Wood
208 x 244 cm
*From the church of
Santo Spirito, Florence
Entered in 1814*

^

Fran Angelico
Vicchio di Mugello (?), circa
1400 (?) – Rome, 1455
*The Coronation
of the Virgin*
Circa 1430/5

Wood
209 x 206 cm

Predella:
*Five scenes from the life
of St Dominic*

Wood
295 x 210 cm
*From the church of the Convent
of San Domenico, Fiesole
Entered in 1814*

**Stefano di Giovanni,
called Sassetta**
Siena, 1392 (?) – 1450
*The Madonna and
Child with six angels*
Wood. 207 x 118 cm

*St Anthony of Padua
St John the Evangelist*
Wood. 195 x 57 cm
(each wing)
*Panels from the altarpiece
of San Francesco, Borgo
San Sepolcro (1437/44)
Purchased in 1956*

>
Paolo Uccello
Florence, 1397 – 1475
*The Battle of San
Romano, circa 1450/6*

Wood. 180 x 316 cm
*Collection of the
Marquis Campana
Purchased
in 1863*

>
**Stefano di
Giovanni,
called Sassetta**
Siena, 1392-
Siena, 1450
*The Damnation
of the soul of the
miser of Citerna*
Circa 1437/44

Wood
45 x 58 cm
Purchased in 1988

^
Piero della Francesca
Borgo San Sepolcro, 1422 (?) –
Borgo San Sepolcro, 1492
Sigismondo Malatesta
Circa 1451

Wood. 44 x 34 cm
Purchased in 1978

>
Alesso Baldovinetti
Florence, circa 1426 – Florence, 1499
The Madonna and Child
Circa 1460/5

Wood. 106 x 75 cm
*Purchased in 1898 with the help
of the Société des Amis du Louvre*

∧
Marco Zoppo
Cento, 1433 –
Venice, 1478
*Madonna and
child with angels*
1455

Wood transferred to canvas
89 x 72 cm
Purchased in 1980

∧
Andrea Mantegna
Isola di Carturo, circa 1430/1 –
Mantua, 1506
St Sebastian
Circa 1480

Canvas
255 x 140 cm
Purchased in 1960

>
Andrea Mantegna
Isola di Carturo, circa 1430/1 –
Mantua, 1506
*Wisdom triumphant
over the Vices*
Circa 1502

Canvas
160 x 92 cm
*From the collection of Isabella
d'Este at Mantua, collection
of the Duc de Richelieu
Entered in 1801*

This panel once formed the central part of the predella of the great altarpiece painted by antegna, then at the height of his powers, for the High Altar of the Church of San Zeno, Verona. In order to represent the drama of the Crucifixion with historical accuracy, Mantegna has attempted a grandiose and archaeologically exact recreation of classic antiquity. The steep perspective through which the rocky landscape is seen is achieved with astonishing virtuosity.

v
Andrea Mantegna
Isola di Carturo, circa 1430/1 –
Mantua, 1506
Calvary
Between 1457 and 1460

Wood
76 x 96 cm
From the church of San Zeno, Verona
Entered in 1798

>
Giovanni Bellini
Venice, circa 1430 –
Venice, 1516
Calvary
Circa 1465/70

Wood
70 x 63 cm
Purchased in 1970

<
Giovanni Bellini
Venice, circa 1430 –
Venice, 1516
Christ's Blessing
Circa 1460

Wood
58 x 46 cm
Purchased in 1912

v
Cosimo Tura
Known in Ferrara
from 1431 to 1495
The Pietà
Circa 1480

Wood
132 x 268 cm
Collection of the Marquis Campana
Purchased in 1863

∧
Antonello da Messina
Messina, circa 1430 –
Messina, 1479
Christ at the column
Circa 1476

Wood
30 x 21 cm
Purchased in 1992

>
Antonello da Messina
Messina, circa 1430 –
Messina, 1479
Portrait of a man,
called *'Il Condottiere'*
1475

Wood
35 x 28 cm
Purchased in 1865

>
Lorenzo di Credi
Florence, circa 1458 –
Florence, 1537
*The Madonna and Child
with St Julian and
St Nicholas of Myra*
Circa 1490/2

Wood
163 x 164 cm
*From the church of Santa Maria
Maddalena dei Pazzi
Entered in 1814*

∧
Filippino Lippi
Prato (?), 1457 (?) –
Florence, 1504
*The swooning of Esther
before Ahasuerus*
Circa 1475

Wood
48 x 132 cm
Purchased in 1972

∨
**Alessandro di Mariano
Filipepi,** *called* **Sandro
Botticelli**
Florence, 1445 – Florence, 1510
*Venus and the Graces
offering gifts to a young girl*
Circa 1430/3

Fresco
212 x 284 cm
Purchased in 1882

>
Carlo Braccesco
Known in Liguria and in
Lombardy from 1478 to 1501
Triptych
Circa 1480/1500

Central panel:
The Annunciation
Wood
158 x 107 cm

Left wing:
*St Benedict and
St Augustine*

Right wing:
St Stephen and St Ange
Wood
105 x 52 cm (each wing)
Purchased in 1812

∧
Vittore Carpaccio
Venice, circa 1460/5 –
Venice, 1525/6
*The sermon of St Stephen
at Jerusalem*
1514 (?)

Canvas
148 x 194 cm
Entered in 1814

>
Cima da Conegliano
Conegliano, 1459/60 –
Conegliano (?), 1517/18
*The Madonna and Child
with St John the Baptist
and Mary Magdalen*
Circa 1510/15

Wood
167 x 110 cm
*From the church of the Convent
of San Domenico, Parma*

The sixteenth century in Italy

The Louvre's collection of Italian High Renaissance paintings is one of its highlights: an irreplaceable treasure with few comparable collections outside Italy.

Its foundations were laid by François I, who set out deliberately to invite to France the most 'modern' artists of the time, the Italian masters. He composed a marvellous gallery of their works, assembled as an example to others and for his own glory as much as for his personal enjoyment. We know that in 1516 he succeeded in attracting the most famous of these artists, Leonardo da Vinci (of whom Louis XII had already been a patron), and reuniting several of his rare paintings; the *Mona Lisa,* the *Madonna of the rocks,* already in the collection of Louis XII, '*La Belle Ferronière*', and the *Virgin and Child with St Anne,* as well as his *St John the Baptist,* which later had to leave the royal collections but was returned in the seventeenth century. He acquired the works of other Florentine artists such as Fra Bartolommeo and Andrea del Sarto (who painted *Charity* during a stay in France in 1518), and he employed Rosso Fiorentino for the decoration of Fontainebleau. It was for François I that Raphael painted *St Michael confounding the Devil* in 1518, as well as the great *Holy Family,* and that Sebastiano del Piombo painted the *Visitation* in 1521. Among other paintings of importance collected by the King (apart from Leonardo and Michelangelo's painting of *Leda,* both mysteriously lost) were '*La Belle Jardinière*' and the *Portrait of the artist with a friend* by Raphael, Guilio Romano's *Joanna of Aragon,* and Savoldo's presumed *Self portrait.* The King also commissioned his portrait in profile from Titian, painted in 1538 after Benvenuto Cellini's medallion.

This basic heritage, kept for a long time at the Château de Fontainebleau and later transferred to the Louvre, was to be considerably enriched when Louis XIV in turn undertook to form a collection whose opulence would illustrate and mirror the brilliance of his reign. The acquisition of part of Cardinal Mazarin's collection in 1661 and of that of the banker Everhard Jabach in 1662-71 brought many superb pictures into the collection. These included Correggio's *Antiope,* the *St Catherine* and the *Allegories* from Isabella d'Este's *studiolo; the Portrait of Balthasar Castiglione,* the small *St George* and the *St Michael* by Raphael; the '*Concert champêtre*' and several other paintings by Titian, notably the *Pardo Venus, The Entombment,* the *Supper at Emmaus,* at *The Man with a glove;* as well as paintings by Veronese and Giulio Romano. Many of these paintings had been bought in London in about 1650 when Charles I's famous collection was dispersed. The King's collection had been, undoubtedly, the finest in Europe at the beginning of the seventeenth century, some of the Italian paintings having come from the Conzaga family collection in Mantua which Charles I had purchased, almost in its entirety, in 1627.

Other Italian Renaissance paintings were soon introduced to Louis XIV's collection: works by Bronzino, Lotto, Pontormo, Palma Vecchio; a series of paintings by Jacopo Bassano which were to decorate one of the rooms of the Grands Appartements of Versailles, but which unfortunately included none of his masterpieces; and more paintings by Veronese, including the vast and superb *Feast at the House of Simon,* offered to the King by the Republic of Venice. During the reign of Louis XV this last painting was incorporated in the decoration of the Salon d'Hercule at Versailles, designed by the architect Robert de Cotte. There were few acquisitions of Italian Renaissance masters under Louis XV and Louis XVI. In 1741 Hyacinthe Rigaud was amongst those who advised the purchase of the *Madonna with a veil* by Raphael and the *Madonna with the green cushion* by Solario from the estate of the Prince de Carignan. When d'Angiviller set up his policy of systematic acquisitions with a view to perfecting the King's collection and making it a public museum he preferred, quite reasonably, to concentrate on schools and periods of art which were less well represented than those of the Italian Renaissance.

The influx of the paintings seized in Italy during the Revolution and the Empire must have made the Louvre into a real 'wonderland' of the Italian Renaissance; but it was to be a fleeting dream. In 1815 representatives from the allied countries took back all the masterpieces from Rome and Florence, and from Parma, Venice, and Bologna, leaving only a handful: the *Paradise* by Tintoretto, the *Holy Family* by Pontormo, the *Crowning with thorns* by Titian, and the *Circumcision* by Barocci, which was left at Notre Dame and not returned to the Louvre until 1862. Also left in exchange for Le Brun's *Feast in the House of Simon,* was the vast *Marriage at Cana* by Veronese. Among the Italian Renaissance works which entered the Louvre during the Revolution and which remained there, were pictures from France itself: works by Mantegna, Costa, and Perugino from Isabella d'Este's collection, seized in 1801 from the Château de Richelieu; the *Mystic marriage of St Catherine* by Bartolommeo from the cathedral of Autun; his *Incredulity of St Thomas* from the Chapelle des Florentins at Lyon; and the *Pietà* by Rosso Fiorentino seized from the chapel of the Château d'Ecouen.

Rich as it may be, the Louvre's collection of Cinquecento paintings clearly has some gaps. We have once again acquired a taste for Mannerist art but it is less well represented than the classicism of the Renaissance, which has proved consistently more popular with French connoisseurs. It is surely significant that the sole work by Parmigianino (recently joined by his delicate but unfinished *Mystic marriage of St Catherine*), a tiny *Portrait of the Artist* from the royal collections, should have had its unusual design radically altered, by enlarging and balancing the composition in order to justify an earlier attribution to Raphael. The most recent purchases of sixteenth-century works have taken account of the need to better illustrate the different cross-currents of the Italian Mannerists, from the movement's origins in Tuscany (as illustrated by Beccafumi's *Predella,* purchased in 1966) through its diffusion in Fontainebleau (*Landscape with the rape of Prosperina* by Nicolo dell'Abbate, bought in 1933) and Prague (Acrimboldo's *Seasons,* bought in 1964) to its use in the pictorial eclecticism of the Counter-Reformation (Antonio Campi, *Scenes from the Passion,* acquired in 1985). It goes without saying, however, that the Louvre will always welcome the unknown works of the great masters as they re-emerge from the depths of obscurity such as Raphael's *Angel* and Lotto's *Christ carrying the cross,* purchased in 1982.

>
Leonardo da Vinci
Vinci, 1452 – Cloux, 1519
St John the Baptist
Circa 1513/15 (?)

Wood
69 x 57 cm
Collection of François I,
collection of Louis XIV

∧
Leonardo da Vinci
Vinci, 1452 – Cloux, 1519
The Madonna of the rocks
1483 (?)

Wood transferred to canvas
199 x 122 cm
Collection of Louis XII (?)

>
Leonardo da Vinci
Vinci, 1452 – Cloux, 1519
The Virgin and Child with
St Anne
Circa 1508/10

168 x 130 cm
Collection of François I,
collection of Louis XIII

<
Leonardo da Vinci
Vinci, 1452 – Cloux, 1519
'La Gioconda',
called *Mona Lisa*
Circa 1503/06

Wood
77 x 53 cm
Collection of François I

>
Fra Bartolommeo
Florence, 1475 –
Florence, 1517
*The Mystic marriage
of St Catherine*
1511

Wood
257 x 228 cm
*From the collegiate church
of Notre Dame, Autun
Entered in 1800*

>
Raffaelo Santi,
called **Raphael and
Giulio Romano**
Urbino, 1483 –
Rome, 1520;
Rome, 1499 –
Mantua, 1546
Joanna of Aragon
1518

Canvas
120 x 96 cm
Collection of François I

∧
Andrea Solario
Milan, circa 1470/5 –
Milan or Pavia, 1524
*The Madonna of
the green cushion*
Circa 1507/10

Wood
60 x 47 cm
*Collection of Louis XV
Purchased in 1742*

>
Raffaello Sanzio, *called* **Raphael**
Urbino, 1483 – Rome, 1520
St George
Circa 1505

Wood. 32 x 27 cm
Collection of Louis XIV. Purchased in 1661

<

Raffaello Sanzio,
called **Raphael**
Urbino, 1483 – Rome, 1520
'La Belle Jardinière',
The Virgin and Child
with St John the Baptist
1507

Wood
122 x 80 cm
Collection of François I (?)

>

Raffaello Sanzio,
called **Raphael**
Urbino, 1483 – Rome, 1520
Balthazar Castiglione
Circa 1514/15

Canvas
82 x 67 cm
Collection of Louis XIV
Purchased in 1661

Popularised by its vivid title, this Virgin and Child with the young St John in a meadow dates from
Raphael's Florentine period and is a mature work inspired by Leonardo and Michelangelo. During
this time the artist painted several variations on the same theme, for example, The Madonna of
the Belvedere *now in Vienna and* The Madonna of the goldfinch *in Florence, always basing his*
design on the perfect balance of a pyramid.

<
Antonio Allegri, *called* Correggio
Correggio, 1489 – Correggio, 1534
The Mystic marriage of St Catherine
Circa 1526/7

Wood
105 x 102 cm
Collection of Louis XIV

∧
Raffaello Sanzio, *called* Raphael
Urbino, 1483 – Rome, 1520
St Michael confounding the Devil
1518

Wood transferred to canvas
268 x 160 cm
Collection of François I

<
Andrea del Sarto
Florence, 1486 – Florence, 1530
The Holy Family
Circa 1515/16

Wood
141 x 106 cm
Collection of François I

^

Antonio Allegri, *called* **Correggio**
Correggio, 1489 – Corregio, 1534
Venus, Satyr, and Cupid, erroneously
called *The Sleep of Antiope*
1524/5

Canvas
190 x 124 cm
Collection of Louis XIV

>
Giacomo Carucci,
called **Pontormo**
Pontormo, 1494 –
Florence, 1556
The Holy Family
Circa 1527/9

Wood
228 x 176 cm
From the Convent of St Anna
at Verzaia, Florence
Entered in 1814

^
Niccolo dell' Abbate
Moderna, circa 1509 or 1512 –
Fontainebleau or Paris, 1571 (?)
The rape of Proserpina
Circa 1560

Canvas
196 x 218 cm
Purchased in 1933

>
Giovanni Battista di Jacopo,
called **Rosso Florentino**
Florence, 1495 –
Fontainebleau, 1540
Pietà
Circa 1530/5

Wood transferred to canvas
125 x 159 cm
Seized during the French Revolution
(collection of Louis-Joseph
de Bourbon, Prince de Condé)

>
Tiziano Vecellio,
called **Titian**
Pieve di Cadore, 1488/9 –
Venice, 1576
Portrait of a man, called
The man with a glove
Circa 1520/3

Canvas
100 x 89 cm
Collection of Louis XIV
Purchased in 1671

v
Tiziano Vecellio,
called **Titian**
Pieve di Cadore, 1488/9 –
Venice, 1576
'Le concert champêtre'
Circa 1510/11

Canvas
110 x 138 cm
Collection of Louis XIV
Purchased in 1671

<
**Tiziano Vecellio,
called Titian**
Pieve di Cadore, 1488/9 –
Venice, 1576
The Crowning with thorns
Circa 1542

Wood
303 x 180 cm
*From Santa Maria
della Grazie, Milan
Entered in 1797*

∧
Sebastiano Del Piombo
Venice (?), circa 1485 –
Rome, 1547
The Visitation
1521

Canvas
168 x 132 cm
Collection of François I

<
Jacomo Palma Vecchio
Serimalta, circa 1480 –
Venice, 1528
*The Adoration
of the Shepherds*
Circa 1515/20

Canvas
140 x 210 cm
*Collection of Louis XIV
Purchased in 1685*

∧
Tiziano Vecellio,
called **Titian**
Pieve di Cadore, 1488/9 –
Venice, 1576
The Entombment
Circa 1525

Canvas
148 x 205 cm
Collection of Louis XIV
Purchased in 1662

This painting was executed in about 1525 for the Gonzagas of Mantua and is on of Titian's supreme classical masterpieces, probably inspired by Raphael's Deposition. *Based on a masterly play of expressive contrasts, notably in the contrast of light and shadow to convey twilight, the composition is an example of the lyrical Venetian Grand Manner and has always been admired and emulated.*

>
**Giovanni Girolamo
Savoldo**
Brescia, circa 1480/5 –
Venice (?), after 1548
Self-portrait, formerly called
Portrait of Gaston de Foix
Circa 1531/2

Canvas
91 x 23 cm
Collection of François I (?)

<
Lorenzo Lotto
Venice, 1480 – Loretto, 1556
Christ bearing the cross
1526

Canvas
66 x 60 cm
Purchased in 1982

>
Lorenzo Lotto
Venice, 1480 –
Loretto, 1556
*St Jerome
in the desert*
1506

Wood
48 x 40 cm
Purchased in 1857

v
Lorenzo Lotto
Venice, 1480 –
Loretto, 1556
*Christ and the woman
taken in adultery*
Circa 1530/5

Canvas
124 x 156 cm
Collection of Louis XIV

∧
Jacopo Robusti, *called* **Tintoretto**
Venice, 1512 – Venice, 1594
Paradise
Circa 1578/9

Canvas
143 x 362 cm
Sketch for the Paradise *of the Great Council*
Room of the Palazzo Ducale in Venice
From the Palazzo Bevilacqua, Verona
Entered in 1799

∧
Paolo Caliari, *called* **Veronese**
Verona, 1528 – Venice, 1588
The Supper at Emmaus
Circa 1559/60

Canvas
290 x 448 cm
Collection of Louis XIV

V
Paolo Caliari,
called **Veronese**
Verona, 1528 – Venice, 1588
The Marriage at Cana
1562/3

Canvas
666 x 990 cm
*From the Convent of San Giorgio
Maggiore, Venice
Entered in 1798*

Federico Barocci
Urbino, circa 1535 –
Urbino, 1612
The Circumcision
1590

Canvas
374 x 252 cm
*From the Church
of the Brotherhood of
the Name of Jesus at Pesaro
Entered in 1798*

To compose this immense painting, destined for Palladio's
Refectory in the Benedictine Convent on San Maggiore in
Venice, Veronese gave free rein to his pictorial imagination.
In a bright architectural setting inspired by Palladio, he
transfigures the religious scene into a lavish worldly banquet.
Careful restoration and the removal of later touching-up and
yellowed varnish have once more revealed the splendours of
Veronese's palette.

The fifteenth and sixteenth centuries in Flanders and Holland

Although it is probable that the collection of François I originally contained works by contemporary Flemish artists – we know Joos van Cleve was at Fontainebleau in about 1530 – nothing original remained in the royal collections.

But not one remained in the royal collections, although they are known by various copies in several museums. When Le Brun drew up an inventory of the King's collection in 1683 he recorded three, or four Flemish paintings of the fifteenth and early sixteenth centuries: the *Wedding at Cana* by Gerard David, then attributed to Jean de Bruges; and, under the name of Holbein, both the *Sacrifice of Abraham,* now attributed to the Brunswick Monogrammist, and the *Portrait of a man* by Joos van Cleve. The paintings by early Flemish masters at the Musée Napoléon included several panels of van Eyck's *Altarpiece of the Mystic Lamb,* taken from Ghent, and the *Virgin of Canon van der Paele,* taken from Bruges, as well as Memling's triptych of *The Last Judgement* from Danzig and the *St Christopher* triptych from Brussels. All these works were returned to their towns of origin in 1816. *The Annunciation* by Rogier van der Weyden, which came from Turin, and the *Madonna of Chancellor Rolin* by Jan van Eyck, from the collegiate church at Autun, have remained in the Louvre. These works excited the curiosity and admiration of young devotees of a return to the Gothic style of painting, like the German philosopher Schlegel and the Boisserée brothers in Cologne, who were to build up a remarkable collection of Flemish an German primitives, now in the Alte Pinakothek at Munich. But the enthusiasm was not yet widespread. Stendhal, faithful to the classical taste for the ideal, if bland, harmonies of the Roman and Bolognese schools, reacted to the popular success of Memling's *Last Judgement* by writing in 1814: 'It's a German School daub… people love to see the grimaces of the damned'. Experts and historians are still confused in their knowledge of this School of painting: van der Weyden's *Annunciation,* like Memling's *Last Judgement,* is sometimes regarded as a German work.

Another notable acquisition of the Musée Napoléon was the purchase in Paris in 1806 of *The banker and his wife* signed by Quentin Metsys. The Restoration and the July Monarchy provided this and many other areas of the collection with few important treasures, although in 1882 '*The pastoral sermon*' (with the church of St Gudule,

Brussels, in the background, which gave its name to the artist) was acquired. On the other hand, the period 1845-1914 saw an uninterrupted series of gifts and purchases. The *Carondelet diptych* by Jan Gossaert, for instance, was bought in 1847. Memling is exceptionally well represented in the Louvre, thanks chiefly to the bequest by the Comtesse Duchatel of the great *Virgin and Child with Jacob Floreins* in 1878 and to the purchase of the *Triptych of the Resurrection* in 1860 and the *Portrait of an old woman* in 1908. At the same time the Flemish primitives section was gaining some measure of consistency with the entry of several works by Dieric Bouts, for example *The Lamentation,* and of paintings by Gerard David, such as the *Sedano triptych,* purchased in 1890, and by Quentin Mersys, Joos van Cleve, Gossaert, Provost, and Bernard van Orley. Works by the Antwerp Mannerists, for example *Lot and his daughters,* for a long time attributed to Lucas van Leyden, and the *Martyrdom of St John* from the Schlichting bequest and in 1914, also supplemented the section. It was at this time that these artists were triumphantly reinstated by a great exhibition in Bruges in 1902, and that their rarity on the market made competition between major museums particularly keen. The keeper of the Louvre succeeded in buying *The Raising of Lazarus* by Geertgen tot Sint Jans and a remarkable work by Rogier van der Weyden, the *Braque triptych* in 1913, but they failed in their attempt to secure a work by Hugo van der Goes, the one great master absent from the collections. There is a story that when his admirable *Adoration of the Magi* was discreetly put up for sale by the monastery of Monforte in Spain in 1914 the envoy of the all-powerful Kaiser Friedrich Museum in Berlin arrived a profitable few days before the agents of the Louvre and acquired the painting.

Since then, paintings by artists previously unrepresented have been acquired for the collection. *The Ship of Fools* by Hieronymus Bosch, was given in 1918 by Camille Benoit, former keeper of the Louvre; the *Christ and the Samaritan woman* by Juan de Flandes, was bought in 1926 and joined forty years later by another small companion panel of the *Coronation of the Virgin,* painted for Queen Isabella by Michel Sittow; *St Jerome* by Joachim Patenier was given by the English dealer Duveen in 1923; the *Pietà* by Petrus Christus was bought in 1951; and *The fortune teller* by Lucas van Leyden came with the Lebaudy bequest in 1962. We should also mention Christian Aulanier's gift in 1973 of the *Christian Allegory,* a rare work by Jan Provost and the purchase in 1989 of *Abraham, Sara and the Angel* by the same artist.

Different criteria were applied for the introduction to the collection of Dutch painters of the second half of the sixteenth century. The paintings of Lambert Sustris – *Venus and Cupid* and *The Baptism of the eunuch* – were in Louis XIV's collection and were appreciated for their affinity to the prestigious Venetian School, whilst the numerous landscapes by Paul Bril were seen as a link with the ideal classical landscapes of Claude and Poussin which he had inspired. The Cabinet du Roi also included Antonio Moro's *Cardinal Granvella's dwarf,* but the greatest Flemish painter of the century, Pieter Brueghel, was not represented in the Louvre until 1892, when Paul Mantz presented the small but extraordinary *The beggars*. Other artistic trends of this period were not appreciated by contemporaries, or indeed at all until recently. When the Duc de Morny gave Jan Massy's *Bathsheba* to the Louvre in 1852 he was accused of ridding himself of a 'complete mediocrity'. It is only thanks to odd donations such as that of Cornelis van Dalem's *Farmyard* (Benoit gift, 1918) and judicious purchases such as *The artist painting with his family* by Otto van Veen, bought in 1835, and *Justice* by Bartholomeus Spranger, bought in 1936, that artistic currents of the late sixteenth century such as Flemish Mannerism are represented in the Louvre at all.

∧

Jan van Eyck
Maaseyck, (?) –
Bruges, 1441
*The Madonna of
Chancellor Rolin*
Circa 1435

Wood
66 x 62 cm
*From the collegiate church
of Notre Dame d'Autun
Entered in 1800*

∨
**Rogier van
der Weyden**
Tournai, 1399/1400 –
Brussels, 1464
*Braque family
triptych*
Circa 1450

Central wing:
*Christ between
the Virgin Mary
and St John
the Evangelist*

Wood
41 x 68 cm

Left wing:
St John the Baptist,

Right wing:
St Mary Magdalen
Wood
41 x 34 cm
(each wing)
Purchased in 1913

^

Rogier van der Weyden
Tournat, 1399/1400 –
Brussels, 1464
The Annunciation
Circa 1435

Wood
86 x 93 cm
From the Royal Gallery, Turin
Entered in 1799

<
Dieric Bouts
Haarlem, circa 1420 –
Louvain, 1475
The Lamentation of Christ
Circa 1460

Wood
69 x 49 cm
Bequeathed by
M Mongé-Misbach, 1871

∧
Geertgen tot Sint Jans
Leiden (?), 1460/5 –
Haarlem, 1488/93
The Raising of Lazarus
Circa 1480

Wood
127 x 97 cm
Purchased in 1902

∧
Hans Memling
Seligenstadt am Main,
circa 1435 – Bruges, 1494
Portrait of an old woman
Circa 1470/5

Wood
35 x 29 cm
Purchased in 1908

**Master of the view
of St Gudule**
Active in Brussels
between 1470 and 1490
The Preaching of St Géry,
called *'The pastoral
sermon',* with the church
of St Gudule, Brussels,
in the background
Circa 1475/80

Wood
98 x 69 cm
Purchased in 1922

>
**Hans Memling
Seligenstadt am Main**
Circa 1435 – Bruges, 1494
*Triptych of the
Resurrection*
Circa 1490

Central panel:
61 x 44 cm

Left wing:
*The Martyrdom
of St Sebastian*

Right wing:
The Ascension

Wood
61 x 18 cm (each wing)
Purchased in 1860

^

Michel Sittow
Reval, circa 1468 –
Reval, 1525/6
*The Coronation
of the Virgin*
Between 1496 and 1504

Wood
24 x 18 cm
Purchased in 1966

<
Juan de Flandes
Known in Castille from 1596 –
Palencia, 1519
*Christ and the Samaritan
woman*
Between 1496 and 1504

Wood
24 x 17 cm
Purchased in 1926

^
Hieronymus Bosch
Bois-le-Duc, circa 1450 –
Bois-le-Duc, 1516
The Ship of Fools
Circa 1500 (?)

Wood
58 x 32 cm
*Presented by Camille Benoit,
1918*

<
Gerard David
Ouwater, 1450/60 –
Bruges, 1523
The marriage at Cana
Circa 1500

Wood
100 x 128 cm
Collection of Louis XIV
Entered before 1683

v
Quentin Metsys
Louvain, 1465/6 –
Antwerp, 1530
The banker and his wife
1514

Wood
70 x 67 cm
Purchased in 1806

>
Jan Gossaert,
called **Mabuse**
Maubeuge (?), circa 1478 –
Middelburg, 1532
Carondolet diptych
1517

Left wing:
Jean Carondolet

Right wing:
Virgin and Child

Curved wood
42 x 27 cm (each wing)
Purchased in 1847

<
Joachim Patenier
Dinant, circa 1480 –
Antwerp, 1524
St Jerome in the desert
Circa 1515 (?)

Wood
78 x 37 cm
*Presented by Sir Joseph
Duveen, 1923*

>
Joos van Cleve
Cleves (?), circa 1485 –
Antwerp, 1540/1
*The Lamentation
of Christ*
Circa 1530

Wood
145 x 204 cm

Central panel
of an altarpiece which
includes a lunette
*(The Stigmatization
of St Francis)*
and a predella
(The Last Supper)

*From the church
of Santa Maria
della Pace, Genoa
Entered in 1813*

^
Lucas van Leyden
Leiden, 1494 – Leiden, 1533
The fortune teller
Circa 1510

Wood
24 x 30 cm
Bequeathed by Madame Pierre
Lebaudy, 1962

<
Anonymous artist
of Antwerp *or* Leiden
First half of the 16th century
Lot and his daughters
Circa 1520

Wood
48 x 34 cm
Purchased in 1900
Previously attributed
to Lucas van Leyden

> **Cornelis van Dalem**
Known in Antwerp between
1545 and 1573/6
Farmyard with a beggar
Circa 1560 (?)

Wood
38 x 53 cm
Presented by Camille Benoit,
1918

< **Master of the**
Martyrdom of St John
Active in Antwerp, circa 1525
The Martyrdom of St John
the Evangelist
Circa 1525

Curved wood
117 x 67 cm
Bequeathed by Baron Basil
de Schlichting, 1914

< **Anthonis Mor**
van Dashorst,
called **Antonio Moro**
Utrecht, 1519 –
Antwerp, 1575
Cardinal Granvella's
dwarf
Circa 1560

Wood
126 x 92 cm
Collection of Louis XIV
Entered before 1683

^
Pieter Bruegel the Elder
Brueghel (?), circa 1525 –
Brussels, 1569
The beggars
1568

Wood
18 x 21 cm
Presented by Paul Mantz, 1892

Although small in scale, this work concisely expresses Bruegel's sarcastic, anguished, but ultimately sympathetic view of the human condition. It has been suggested both that he is depicting a simple scene of the departure of the lepers of Lazaretto for a carnival, and that the cripples have a political, sociological, or moral significance, but in either case the artist gives a powerful impression of the physical misery and the moral isolation of these outcasts.

\>
Lambert Sustris
Amsterdam, between 1515
and 1520 – Padua (?),
after 1568
Venus and Cupid
Circa 1560 (?)

Canvas
132 x 184 cm
Collection of Louis XIV
Entered before 1683

v
Jan Massys
Antwerp, circa 1509 –
Antwerp, circa 1575
David and Bathsheba
1562

Wood
162 x 197 cm
Presented by the
Comte du Morny, 1852

The seventeenth century in Flanders

The first Flemish paintings to enter the royal collection in the seventeenth century were by living artists who had been brought to work in Paris by Marie de Médicis.

Frans Pourbus painted the Queen's official portrait for the Petite Galerie of the Louvre and some large religious canvases for churches, including *The Last Supper*, which was seized during the Revolution. Rubens, the famous Antwerp master, was commissioned by the Queen Mother to paint the decorations for the Long Gallery of the Palais du Luxembourg, inaugurated in 1625 for the marriage of Henrietta of France with Charles I of England. It consisted of twenty-four canvases illustrating and, of course, glorifying episodes in the life of the Queen from her birth in Florence to her reconciliation with her son Louis XIII. Historical facts, both real and slightly imaginary; are mingled with allegory in a vast sensual display, which represents the very summit of Baroque painting. Yet at the time it seems to have struck few chords, as the Parisian taste of the mid-century was attuned to Italian classicism and its sober French interpretation.

It was not until the decade 1660-70 that Flemish paintings entered the royal collections once again. Although they were unimportant in Mazarin's collection, acquired in 1661, the Flemish paintings from the Jabach collection are excellent and include masterpieces by Rubens (*Thomyris and Cyrus* and *The Virgin with Saint Innocent* and by van Dyck (the Palatine Princes). In Parisian artistic circles battle had already been joined between the partisans of colour, the Rubénistes, and the Poussinistes, who upheld, in the name of classicism, the merits of strict draughtsmanship. Roger de Piles brought the qualities of Rubens to light and the Médicis galleries found new admirers. Collections of Flemish paintings multiplied and the royal collection was enriched with new paintings by van Dyck, the *Virgin with donors* and *Venus and Vulcan,* and by Rubens, including *The kermis* bought in 1685 from M. de Hauterive, and with many decorative landscapes by Paul Bril and Joos de Momper. Jan Brueghel the Elder's masterpiece, the *Battle of Issus,* was left to Louis XIV by Le Nôtre in 1693.

Whilst many private collections, foremost of which was the incomparable collection of the Duc d'Orléans, were begun or developed during the Regency and the reign of Louis XV, the Cabinet du Roi increased very little. At least the few acquisitions were of the highest quality: Rubens' *The flight of Lot,* bought from the estate of the Prince de Carignan (1741), the *Seven works of mercy,* the first important painting by Teniers in the royal collection, the *Calvary* by van Dyck, then attributed to Rubens (from the Jesuit church of Bergues St Winnocq, 1749), and *Christ driving the merchants from the temple* by Jordaens, given in 1751 by the painter Charles Joseph Natoire.

Flemish painting was a major feature of the Comte d'Angiviller's programme of acquisition. Bought direct from private collectors, from dealers (especially Le Brun), or from public sales, the paintings he assembled formed an intelligent complement to the original collection. They provided a better illustration of genre painting in the works of Craesbeck and Teniers and of religious paintings on a grand scale by Rubens' *The Martyrdom of St Liévin,* bought at the sale of the church of the Flanders Jesuits and sent to the museum in Brussels in 1803, and his *Adoration of the magi.* The paintings also improved the representation of Jordaens, *The Four Evangelists,* of van Dyck, with his *Charles I,* bought in 1775 from Madame du Barry, and of Rubens the portraitist with *Helena Fourment and his children,* purchased at the Comte de Vaudreuil's sale in 1784.

The seizure of treasures from the nobility at the time of the Revolution ensured the acquisition of genre paintings and small format collectors' pieces (Francken, Teniers, Neeffs) and of still lifes (Snyders, Fyt) which were plentiful in Parisian collections. It also claimed large religious and mythological canvases, such as *St Macarius of Ghent* by Jacob van Oost, seized from the Prince de Conti and *Hercules and Omphale* by Rubens, which were all that remained when the Galerie d'Orléans was exported wholesale to England. Of the paintings taken from Flanders during the Revolution, including works such as the *Descent from the Cross* or the *'Coup de Lance'* by Rubens, nearly all were returned to their country of origin in 1815. After this dramatic reflux the desolated walls of the Louvre had to be rehung: a noteworthy solution was the return of the Marie de Médicis cycle by Rubens from the Musée du Luxembourg.

On the other hand, the period of the Second Empire was particularly extravagant as the La Caze donation in 1869 consisted of more than seventy paintings. These included still lifes by Fyt and Snyders, a series of paintings by Teniers, paintings by van Dyck such as the *Martyrdom of St Sebastian* and, most important of all, a series of sketches by Rubens, *Philopoemen recognised* and sketches for the ceiling of the church of the Anwerp Jesuits. These had been chosen for their dazzling freedom of execution by Dr La Caze, who was an ardent admirer of Watteau and Fragonard.

Most of the Flemish paintings which have entered the Louvre in the last hundred years have done so thanks to private generosity. For instance, *The standard-bearer* by Victor Boucquet, the *Twilight landscape* by Adriaen Brouwer, and the great *Ixion tricked by Juno* were part of the Schlichting bequest in 1914. *The death of Dido* by Rubens and the *Portrait of a gentleman* by van Dyck were amongst the very fine paintings given by Carlos de Beistegui in 1942. The van Dyck collection was lacking one of his great portraits of the Genoese aristocracy, and this gap was filled by the gift of a *Portrait of the Marchesa Spinola Doria* in 1949 by Baron Edouard de Rothschild's heirs. Rubens' *Portrait of Helena Fourment with a carriage* came from the same collection, in payment of capital transfer tax. As active as ever, the Société des Amis du Louvre presented the museum with *Diana resting* by Jordaens and gave generously towards the purchase of the *Resurrection of Christ* by Gerard Seghers in 1990.

>
Paul Bril
Antwerp, 1554 – Rome, 1626
The stag hunt
Circa 1595/1600 (?)

Canvas
105 x 137 cm
Collection of Louis XIV
Entered before 1683

v
Jan Brueghel the Elder,
called 'Velvet Brueghel'
Brussels, 1568 – Antwerp, 1625
The Battle of Issus
1602

Wood
86 x 135 cm
Collection of Louis XIV, bequeathed
to the King by Le Nôtre, 1693

<
Jacob Jordaens
Antwerp, 1593 –
Antwerp, 1678
The repose of Diana
Circa 1645-55

Canvas
203 x 264 cm
*Presented by the Société
des Amis du Louvre, 1982*

v
Peter Paul Rubens
Siegen, 1577 –
Antwerp, 1640
*The Apotheosis of Henri IV
and the proclamation
of the regency of Marie
de Médicis on 14 May 1610*
Circa 1622/4

Canvas
394 x 727 cm
*Collection of Louis XIV
Entered in 1693*

∧
Peter Paul Rubens
Siegen, 1577 – Antwerp, 1640
The kermis
Circa 1635

Wood
149 x 261 cm
Collection of Louis XIV
Acquired in 1685

∨
Peter Paul Rubens
Siegen, 1577 – Antwerp, 1640
*Philopoemen, General of
the Achaeans, recognized by
the old woman of Megara*
Circa 1610

Wood
50 x 66 cm
Bequeathed by Louis La Caze, 1869

∧

Jacob Jordaens
Antwerp, 1593 –
Antwerp, 1678
The Four Evangelists
Circa 1625

Canvas
134 x 118 cm
Collection of Louis XVI
Purchased in 1784

>
Jacob Jordaens
Antwerp, 1593 –
Antwerp, 1678
*Christ driving the
merchants from
the Temple*
Circa 1650

Canvas
288 x 436 cm
*Collection of Louis XV
Purchased in 1751*

∧
Victor Boucquet
Furnes, 1619 – Furnes, 1677
The standard-bearer
1664

Canvas
184 x 112 cm
*Presented by the Comtesse
de Comminges-Guitaud, 1898*

>
Adriaen Brouwer
Audenarde, 1605/6 –
Antwerp, 1638
Twilight landscape
Circa 1633/7

Wood
17 x 26 cm
Presented by M Friedsam, 1926

v
David Teniers
Antwerp, 1610 – Brussels, 1690
*Heron hunting with the Archduke
Leopold Wilhelm*
Circa 1650/60

Canvas
82 x 120 cm
*Collection of Louis XVI
Purchased in 1784*

<
Jacob van Oost the Younger
Bruges 1637 – Bruges, 1713
*St Macarius of Ghent giving
and to the plague victims*
1673

Canvas
350 x 257 cm
*Seized during the French Revolution
(collection of the Prince de Conti)*

>
Jan Fyt
Antwerp, 1611 – Antwerp, 1661
*Game and hunting gear
discovered by a cat*
Circa 1640/50 (?)

Canvas
95 x 122 cm
Bequeathed by Louis La Caze, 1869

The seventeenth century in Holland

Official taste for history painting had long prevented the admiration of the contemporary Dutch masters, who painted mainly supposedly 'inferior' subjects devoted to the representation of everyday life.

The pre-eminence accorded to history painting by the Académie Royale de Peinture et de Sculpture placed it at the summit of the hierarchy of acceptable subject matter in seventeenth-century France. Several Dutch Italiante landscapists, such as Jan Asselijn or Herman van Swanevelt, who painted landscapes for the decoration of the Hôtel Lambert (which entered the royal collection under Louis XVI), were appreciated in France at this time, but this was undoubtedly because they were linked to the tradition of ideal classical landscape painting. Rembrandt was not well known in France during his life-time; people were disconcerted by his technique, 'which often seems nothing but a rough sketch', according to the contemporary architect and critic Félibien des Araux, even when they were not shocked by his 'bad taste'. A diplomatic gift to the King from Maurice of Nassau in 1678/9, the series of *Views of Brazil* by Frans Post, today appreciated for their simple charm, was considered not so much great art, but rather as a document prized for its exoticism, and was duly consigned to the Cabinet des Curiosités. It is not surprising, however, to find among Louis XIV's purchases the great *Still life* by Davidsz de Heem, a foretaste of the sumptuous decorative displays by Monnoyer and Desportes, and later an inspiration to Matisse, who made two copies.

The first indication of a change of sensibility was the entry into the King's collection in 1671, just two years after the artist's death, of the *Portrait of the artist* of 1600 by Rembrandt. The purchase of several works by Gerard Dou (including *The Bible reading*) between 1684 and 1715 marks a more significant turning-point. From then on French collectors, struck by Flemish painting, also sought landscapes, still lifes, and Dutch genre scenes in which they appreciated the 'truth of life', the delicacy of execution, and the artful light effects. Soon the fashion had spread among a number of young Dutch painters working 'in the style of Rembrandt'. Throughout the eighteenth century it was expressed in the collection of a considerable number of Dutch paintings of the previous century, whose reduced dimensions suited the décor of the smaller rooms then in vogue in France. We should underestimate the relationship in feeling and pictorial taste which links so many of the great French painters, from Chardin and Oudry to Fragonard and Greuze, to their Dutch predecessors.

In 1742 the royal collection was enriched by the acquisition of several fine paintings from the estate of the Prince de Carignan, including Rembrandt's *The Angel Raphael leaving Tobias*. It was under Louix XVI that the most decisive purchases were made, either through the agency of dealers like Le Brun, who supplied the *Soldier offering money to a woman* by Ter Borch and *The departure for the ride* by Cuyp, or at public sales. At Randon de Boisset's sale in 1777, *The Supper at Emmaus* by Rembrandt was

<

Jan Vermeer
Delft, 1632 – Delft, 1675
The lacemaker
Circa 1665

Canvas applied to wood
24 x 21 cm
Purchased in 1870

bought, and at the Comte de Vaudreuil's sale in 1784 the *Two philosophers* (one now attributed to Samuel Koninck) and the *Portrait of Hendrickje Stoffels* by Rembrandt, as well as *The Ray of sunlight* by Jacob Ruisdael, were purchased.

Parisian collections were quite infatuated with Dutch painting, and there is not better proof of this than the lists of paintings seized from the emigrés. To mention but a few, there are *St Matthew and the Angel* by Rembrandt, his later version of *The Supper at Emmaus* and two self-portraits, the *Adoration of the Shepherds* by Bloemaert, and *The concert* by Ter Borch. Meanwhile, French painting at the end of the eighteenth century was also affected: Boilly, Marguerite Gérard, and Drolling revived the style of Metsu and Dou, while Demarne and Swebach imitated Wouwerman or Berchem.

Several interesting additions mark the period of the Revolution and the Empire, notably that of the famous *The dropsical woman* by Dou, given by Charles Emmanuel of Savoy in 1799. From the Stathouder collection, transferred to Paris in 1795, all that remained in 1815 after the allies had retrieved their paintings were *The concert* by Honthorst and some pictures by Berchem, Wouwerman, and Weenix. Appreciation of the Dutch masters in the nineteenth century was found in many quarters. Some of Balzac's descriptions reflect the fervent admiration later expressed by Fromentin in his *Maîtres d'Autrefois* (1876) or the praise of the artists of the Netherlands offered by Théodore Rousseau, Courbet, Manet, and Redon. The second half of the century enjoyed the fruits of this general admiration with a series of purchases or gifts to the Louvre. *The flayed ox* by Rembrandt was purchased in 1857, and certain artists who had been ignored for years were represented for the first time. Vermeer, whose reputation had been resuscitated by the French critic Gustave Thoré in 1866 was entered with *The lacemaker,* and Hobbema was represented with *The water-mill.* Unfortunately, artists such as Philip Konick or Jan van de Capelle, who were appreciated by British collectors, did not benefit in this way.

The Dutch paintings of the La Caze bequest in 1869 are, like all those of this infallible connoisseur, of the finest quality. Paintings by Ter Borch, van Ostade, Steen, and van Goyen are dominated by three masterpieces; the incomparable *Bathsheba* by Rembrandt, the *The gipsy girl* and the *Portrait of a woman* by Frans Hals. Besides important individual donations, international gifts of entire collections at the beginning of this century much increased the Dutch section. The Schlichting bequest in 1914, and particularly the Comte de l'Espine's collection of 1930, which included the mysterious *Pair of slippers* now attributed to Samuel van Hoogstraten, were the most important of these gifts.

Recent years, though less prolific, have seen the enrichment and diversification of the collection with the addition of famous masterpieces by the three greatest painters of the century, Rembrandt, Hals and Vermeer. Several purchases and gifts show the need to represent artists (Aert de Gelder, Carel Fabritius, Ter Brugghen, Coorte Sweerts, Saenredam, Bramer), movements (the Mannerism of Wtewael and Cornelius of Haarlem, illustrated by the two major works presented by the Société des Amis du Louvre), genres such as still life (Bosschaert) or aspects of the work of certain masters (*Still life* by Salomon Ruisdael and Flick's *Landscape*) which have finally been given the prominence they deserve by today's historians. Among the gifts, three major pieces stand out: the *Portrait of Titus* and the *Castle* which completes the Rembrandt collection with the addition of one of his rare landscapes (Nicolas gift, 1948) and the *A young woman drinking* by Pieter de Hooch (gift of Madame Piatigorsky, 1974), which came from the collection of Baron Alphonse de Rothschild. From the same collection, Vermeer's famous *Astronomer* is one of the finest additions to the Louvre since the last war. This work was given to the museum in lieu of death duties, as was another Dutch masterpiece, the *Clown with a lute* by Frans Hals.

>
Ambrosius Boschaert
Antwerp, 1573 – Middleburg, 1621
Bouquet of flowers
Circa 1620

Copper
23 x 17 cm
Purchased with the assistance of
the Société des Amis du Louvre, 1984

∨
Joachim Wtewael
Utrecht, 1566 – Utrecht, 1638
Perseus and Andromeda
1611

Canvas
180 x 150 cm
Presented by the Société
des Amis du Louvre, 1982

<
Getrit van Honthorst
Utrecht, 1590 – Utrecht, 1656
The concert
1624

Canvas
168 x 178 cm
*From the Stadhouder
collection, the Hague
Entered in 1795*

V
Abraham Bloemaert
Gorkum, 1564 – Utrecht, 1651
Adoration of the Shepherds
1612

Canvas
287 x 229 cm
*From the Milliotty collection
Entered in 1799*

<
Hendrick ter Brugghen
Deventer, 1588 – Utrecht, 1629
The duet, 1628

Canvas
106 x 82 cm
Purchased in 1954

>
Pieter Jansz Saenredam
Assendelft, 1597 –
Haarlem, 1665
*Interior of the church
of Saint-Bavon, Haarlem*
1630

Canvas
41 x 37 cm
Purchased in 1983

<
Salomon van Ruysdael
Naarden, 1600/3 –
Haarlem, 1670
Still life with a turkey
1661

Canvas
112 x 85 cm
Purchased in 1965

>
Jan van Goyen
Leiden, 1596 –
The Hague, 1656
*River-landscape with
a windmill and
a ruined castle*
1644

Canvas
97 x 133 cm
Collection of Louis XVI

With this portrait of a jovial gipsy wench, Hals continues in the Caravaggesque tradition of popular subjects which was imported from Rome by Terbrugghen and Honthorst. However, it is the exuberance of the light and colourful brushstrokes of his technique which conveys the sensation of spontaneity and life in this painting. The actual handling of the paint has now become a means of expression in itself.

∧
Frans Hals
Antwerp, circa 1581/5 –
Haarlem, 1666
The gipsy girl
Circa 1628/30

Wood
58 x 52 cm
Bequeathed by
Louis La Caze, 1869

Frans Hals
Antwerp, circa 1581/5 –
Haarlem, 1666
Portrait of a woman
Circa 1650 (?)

Canvas
108 x 80 cm
*Bequeathed by Louis La Caze,
1869*

v

Frans Hals
Antwerp, circa 1581/5 –
Haarlem, 1666
Clown with a lute
Circa 1620-25

Canvas
70 x 62 cm
*Given in lieu of
transfer duty, 1984*

This painting, one of the artist's most famous works, is from the Caravaggesque period of Frans Hals (around 1620-1625), from which the Bohemian and other realistic figures also date: figures which are astonishing masterpieces of naturalist force and painterly brilliance. These works were much admired in nineteenth-century France, especially by the realists and by Manet.

^

**Harmensz Rembrandt
van Rijn**
Leiden, 1606 –
Amsterdam, 1669
The Supper at Emmaus
1648

Wood
68 x 65 cm
*Collection of Louis XVI
Purchased in 1777*

Rembrandt returned several times to the theme of the Supper at Emmaus, which explores the double nature of Christ, His humanity and His essential divinity. Rembrandt interpreted the theme in a different way each time; the composition of this version relies on Italian Renaissance examples and is one of the artist's most serenely classical masterpieces.

∧
**Harmensz Rembrandt
van Rijn**
Leiden, 1606 –
Amsterdam, 1669
*Portrait of the artist
at his easel*
1660

Canvas
111 x 90 cm
*Collection of Louis XIV
Purchased in 1671*

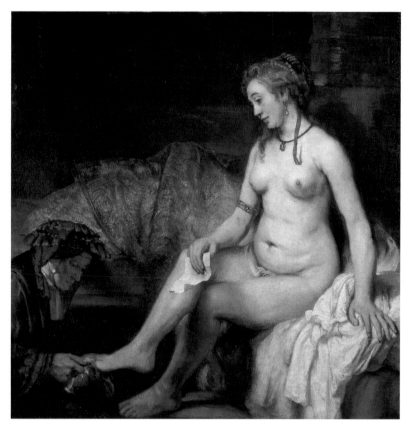

>
**Harmensz Rembrandt
van Rijn**
Leiden, 1606 –
Amsterdam, 1669
The flayed ox
1655

Wood
94 x 69 cm
Purchased in 1857

∧
**Harmensz
Rembrandt van Rijn**
Leiden, 1606 –
Amsterdam, 1669
Bathsheba
1654

Canvas
142 x 142 cm
*Bequeathed by Louis
La Caze, 1869*

>
Govaert Flinck
Clèves, 1615 –
Amsterdam, 1660
Landscape
1637

Wood
49 x 75 cm
Purchased in 1985

>
Gerard Dou
Leiden, 1613 – Leiden, 1675
The dropsical woman
1663 (?)

Wood
86 x 67 cm
Presented by Charles Emmanuel IV
of Savoy to General Clauzel
for the Louvre, 1799

v
Adriaen van Ostade
Haarlem, 1610 –
Haarlem, 1685
Portrait of a family
1654

Wood
70 x 88 cm
Collection of Louis XVI
Purchased in 1785

<
Nicholaes Berchem
Haarlem, 1620 –
Amsterdam, 1683
Landscape with Jacob,
Rachel, and Leahe
1643 (?)

Canvas
166 x 138 cm
Purchased in 1816

>
Cornelis van Poelenburgh
Utrecht, circa 1586 –
Utrecht, 1667
Ruins of ancient Rome
Circa 1620

Copper
44 x 57 cm
Seized during the French Revolution
(collection of the Duchesse
de Noailles)

∨
Aelbrecht Cuyp
Dordrecht, 1620 –
Dordrecht, 1691
Landscape near Rhenen
Circa 1650/5

Canvas
170 x 229 cm
Collection of Louis XVI
Purchased in 1783

v
v
Jan Baptist Weenix
Amsterdam, 1621 –
Utrecht, circa 1660
*Departure of
an oriental entourage*
Circa 1658/60

Canvas
123 x 175 cm
*Collection of Louis XVI
Purchased in 1783*

>
Karel Dujardin
Amsterdam, 1621/2 –
Venice, 1678
*Italian landscape with
herdsmen and a piebald horse*
Circa 1675 (?)

Wood
32 x 27 cm
*Seized during the French Revolution
(collection of Baron de Breteuil)*

∧
Michiel Sweerts
Brussels, 1624 – Goa, 1664
The young man and the procuress
Circa 1660 (?)

Copper. 19 x 27 cm
Purchased in 1967

∨
Jacob Ruisdael
Haarlem, 1628/9 – Amsterdam, 1682
The ray of sunlight
Circa 1660 (?)

Canvas. 83 x 99 cm
Collection of Louis XVI
Purchased in 1784

∨
Davidsz de Heem
Utrecht, 1606 – Antwerp, 1683/4
A table of desserts, 1640

Canvas. 149 x 203 cm
Collection of Louis XIV
Purchased before 1683

>
Jan van der Heyden
Gorkum, 1637 –
Amsterdam, 1712
*The Dam with the new
town hall at Amsterdam*
1668

Canvas
73 x 86 cm
Collection of Louis XVI
Purchased in 1783

v
Gabriel Metsu
Leiden, 1620 –
Amsterdam, 1667
*The Amsterdam
vegetable market*

Canvas
97 x 84 cm
Collection of Louis XVI
Purchased in 1783

>
Meindert Hobbema
Amsterdam, 1638 –
Amsterdam, 1709
The water-mill
Circa 1660/70 (?)

Canvas
80 x 66 cm
Purchased in 1861

This work dates from Pieter de Hooch's best period, 1654-62, when he worked in Delft. During these years he painted tranquil scenes of bourgeois domesticity and conversation pieces set in clearly lit interiors, courtyards, or small gardens. His subtle construction of space in depth and his refined use of lighting create an almost lyrical effect, and his style directly anticipates that of Vermeer.

∧
Gerard ter Broch
Zwolle, 1617 –
Deventer, 1681
The concert
Circa 1657

Wood
47 x 44 cm
*Seized during the French
Revolution (collection of
the Duc de Brissac)*

>
Pieter de Hooch
Rotterdam, 1629 –
Amsterdam, 1684
A young woman drinking
1658

Canvas
69 x 60 cm
*Presented by Mme Piatigorsky,
née Rothschild, 1974*

Λ
Jan Vermeer
Delft, 1632 – Delft, 1675
The astronomer
1668

Canvas
51 x 45 cm
*Given in lieu of transfer
duty, 1983*

Spain

At the time of Louis XIV the French royal collections contained extremely few Spanish paintings.

Only *The Burning Bush* **by Francisco Collantes and the** *Portrait of the young Infanta Margarita* **by Velasquez (or, according to some critics, his studio).** This was the only work of quality among the family portraits with which Queen Anne of Austria, sister of Philip IV, decorated her Cabinet des Bains in the Palais du Louvre. Under Louis XVI some paintings by Murillo, including one of his masterpieces, *The young beggar,* were purchased from the dealer Le Brun. During the eighteenth century the painters of the Golden Age of Spanish painting had made only a modest impression on the great European collections; only Murillo was really sought after, and this preference was to eclipse the qualities of Velasquez for many years.

During the first half of the nineteenth century a great change in attitude took place, and Spain and Spanish art became fashionable. It was not only the Spain of romance and folklore, with its violent contrasts, which fasinated writers, musicians, and lovers of the 'picturesque' alike, but it was also the Spain of the painters of the Golden Age whose dark and passionate works impressed many young artists of the mid-century who had tired of Romanticism and were anxious to escape the empty rhetoric of the Academy.

The influx of Spanish paintings into France during this period was a manifestation of this Hispanicism. Many important new collections were formed, the earliest being brought back from Spain by various generals at the time of Joseph Bonaparte and the War of Independence. Political circumstances favoured the creation of some collections, such as the famous collection of Maréchal Soult. Later, others were assembled with regular and important purchases, helped, from 1835, by the suppression of the religious orders (L'Esclaustracion) and the rumblings of the Carlist War. Among these was the collection of the financier Aguado, as well as the prodigious Spanish collection of Louis-Philippe, which was created after some intelligent prospecting throughout Spain by Baron Taylor. It contained hundreds of works by all the Spanish masters, with particularly brilliant examples of the art of Zurbaran and Goya, and it was exhibited at the Louvre from 1838-48.

Unfortunately, very few of these paintings remain in the Louvre. The pictures sent from Spain for the Musée Napoléon in 1813 were returned two years later. After the 1848 Revolution the Spanish collection was given back to the Orléans family (although one primitive painting was left, forgotten, in store, only to be recognised in recent years as a work by the Catalan master Huguet). This unique, but short-lived, collection was sold in London in 1853 and is now dispersed in museums all over the

<
José de Ribera
Jativa, 1591– Naples, 1652
The club-footed boy
1642

Canvas
164 x 93 cm
*Bequeathed by Louis La Caze,
1869*

world. However, one masterpiece from the Spanish collection has been returned to the Louvre: El Greco's *Christ on the Cross,* purchased in 1908. Negotiations under Louis-Philippe to buy the collection of Maréchal Soult ended in failure, but the Louvre managed to purchase several very important paintings in 1858 and 1867: *St Basil* by Herrera, *The angels' kitchen* and *The Birth of the Virgin* by Murillo, the two great *Scenes from the life of St Bonaventura,* and the small *St Apollonia* by Zurbaran. When part of the collection was sold publicly in 1852, the Louvre managed to buy the famous *Immaculate Conception* by Murillo by raising the bidding to the vast sum of 586,000 francs. In 1940 it went to the Prado as part of an exchange.

In 1865 the first painting by Goya entered the Louvre, his *Portrait of Ferdinand Guillemardet,* painted when the sitter was French Ambassador in Madrid (1798) and bequeathed by his son. It was the first in a series of Goya's portraits gradually acquired by the Louvre, which undoubtedly has the finest such collection outside Spain, containing *The lady with a fan* and *Perez de Castro,* purchased in 1902 and 1858 respectively, the *Marquesa de la Solana,* justly considered to be one of Goya's finest female portraits and acquired through the generosity of Carlos de Beistegui, and the *Marquesa de Santa Cruz,* recently acquired in lieu of death duties.

During the second half of the nineteenth century and the first years of the twentieth century, the acquisitions of paintings of the Golden Age were less numerous than might have been hoped. However, the *Club-footed boy* by Ribera was part of the La Caze donation and El Greco's *St Louis* was acquired in 1903, shortly before his *Christ on the Cross.*

At that time the keepers concentrated their efforts on the primitive painters who were just beginning to be rediscovered. The *Scenes from the Life of St George,* later identified as by the Catalan painter Martorell, were bought in 1904 and 1905, as well as *The investing of St Ildefonso with the chasuble* by a Hispano-Flemish artist from Castile, and three panels from a Valencian polyptych of the fifteenth century from the cathedral of Burgo de Osma. These pictures constitute, together with Huguet's altarpiece of *The flagellation of Christ,* painted for Barcelona Cathedral, a room of rare quality almost unmatched outside Spain.

More recent acquisitions have provided a welcome variety in the collection by introducing significant works by sixteenth-century masters, such as the *Calvary* by the hispanised Brussels painter, Campana, and those of the seventeenth century hitherto absent from the collections. Louis Trista, Juan Valdes Leal, Vicente Carducho, Alonso Cano, and Jeronimo Jacinto Espinosa – or by evoking, albeit insufficiently, the eighteenth century, for example in Melendez's *Portrait of the artist* and *Still life.* Certain series have been completed: two canvases by Herrera from the Church of St Bonaventura in Seville, given by the Société des Amis du Louvre, have joined those by Zurbaran, while another episode from the cycle by Murillo from the Franciscan church at Seville has joined *The angels' kitchen.* Of all these treasures, apart from the works of Goya, the spectacular *Mass for the foundation of the Order of Trinitarians,* painted by Carreño de Miranda in 1666 for the Trinitarians of Pamplona and given by the Comtesse de Caraman in 1964, is without doubt the most magnificent.

>
Master of St Ildefonso
Castile, end of the 15th century
The blessing of the chasuble
to St Ildefonso
Circa 1490-1500

Wood
230 x 167 cm
Purchased in 1904

<
Bernardo Martorell
Known in Barcelona from 1427 to 1452
The flagellation of St George
Circa 1435

Wood
107 x 53 cm
Presented by the Société des Amis du Louvre, 1904

v
Jaime Huguet
Valls, 1414 – Barcelona, 1491
The Flagellation of Christ
Between 1450 and 1460

Wood. 106 x 210 cm
Purchased in 1967 with the help
of the Société des Amis du Louvre

>

Domenikos Theotocopoulos, *called* **El Greco**
Candia, 1541 –
Toledo, 1614
St Louis, King of France and a page

Canvas
120 x 96 cm
Acquired in 1903

Pedro Berruguete
Paredes de Nava, circa 1450 –
Paredes de Nava, 1504
Plato
Circa 1477

Wood
101 x 69 cm
Collection of the Marquis Campana
Purchased in 1863

>

Pietr de Kempeneer, *known as* **Pedro Campaña**
Brussels, 1503 –
Brussels, 1580
Crucifixion
Circa 1550

Canvas backed by wood
54 x 39 cm
Purchased in 1986

<
**Domenikos
Theotocopoulos,**
called **El Greco**
Candia, 1541 –
Toledo, 1614
*Christ on the Cross
adored by donors*
Between 1576
and 1579

Canvas
260 x 171 cm
Purchased in 1908

∧
Francisco de Zurbaran
Fuente de Cantos, 1598 –
Madrid, 1664
*The lying-in-state
of St Bonaventura*
Circa 1629

Canvas
245 x 220 cm
Purchased in 1858

The Louvre owns another painting by Zurbaran, St Bonaventura at the
Council of Lyon, *as well as two by Francisco de Herrera which belongs to
a series painted for the Franciscan college of St Bonaventura at Seville.
During 'The Golden Age' the crusading faith of the great monastic orders
multiplied the number of cycles illustrating the lives and miracles of
popular saints, Through the low-key colouring and sombre subject matter,*
tenebrismo, *derived from Caravaggio, Zurbaran here rediscovers the
intense simplicity of the primitives.*

>
**Francisco Herrera
the Elder**
Seville, circa 1585 –
Madrid, after 1657
*St Basil dictating
his doctrine*
Circa 1639

Canvas
243 x 194 cm
Purchased in 1858

∧
Alonso Cano
Granada, 1601 –
Granada, 1667
St John the Evangelist
1636

Canvas
53 x 35 cm
Purchased in 1977

>
José de Ribera
Jativa, 1591 – Naples, 1652
*The Adoration
of the Shepherds*
1630

Canvas
239 x 181 cm
*Given to the French Republic
by the King of Naples in 1802
in compensation for the paintings
taken by Neapolitan troops
at St-Louis-des-Français*

∧
Juan Carreño de Miranda
Gijon, 1614 – Madrid, 1685
*The mass for the foundation
of the Order of the Trinitarians*
1666

Canvas
500 x 331 cm
*Presented by the Comtesse
de Caraman, 1964*

∨
Francisco Collantes
Madrid (?), circa 1599 –
Madrid (?), 1656
The Burning Bush
Circa 1634

Canvas
116 x 163 cm
Collection of Louis XIV

∨
**Bartolomé Esteban
Murillo**
Seville, 1618 – Seville, 1682
The Birth of the Virgin
Between 1655 and 1658

Canvas
179 x 349 cm
Purchased in 1858

This work was painted at the beginning of Murillo's career. It is without doubt one of the first of the genre scenes in which he shows street urchins. Later his taste for the picturesque sometimes became merely anecdotal, but here the sincerity of his observation and the vigour of his technique place Murillo in the pure tradition of the Spanish tenebrismo of the young Velasquez and of Zurbaran. It is not surprising that painters like Courbet, Manet, and Monet admired such works.

∧
Bartolomé Esteban Murillo
Seville, 1618 – Seville, 1682
The young beggar
Circa 1650

Canvas
134 x 110 cm
Collection of Louis XVI
Purchased in 1782

>
**Francisco Goya
y Lucientes**
Fuendetodos, 1746 –
Bordeaux, 1828
Ferdinand Guillemardet
1798

Canvas
186 x 124 cm
*Bequeathed by Louis
Guillemardet, 1865*

∧
**Francisco Goya
y Lucientes**
Fuendetodos, 1746 –
Bordeaux, 1828
Lady with a fan
Circa 1805/10

Canvas
103 x 83 cm
Purchased in 1898

>
Luis Melendez
Naples, 1716 –
Madrid, 1780
Still life
Circa 1760/70

Canvas
40 x 51 cm
*Bequeathed by Emile
Wauters, 1934*

∧
Francisco Goya y Lucientes
Fuendetodos, 1746 – Bordeaux, 1828
The Marquesa de la Solana
Circa 1793

Canvas
181 x 122 cm
Presented by Carlos de Beistegui, 1942

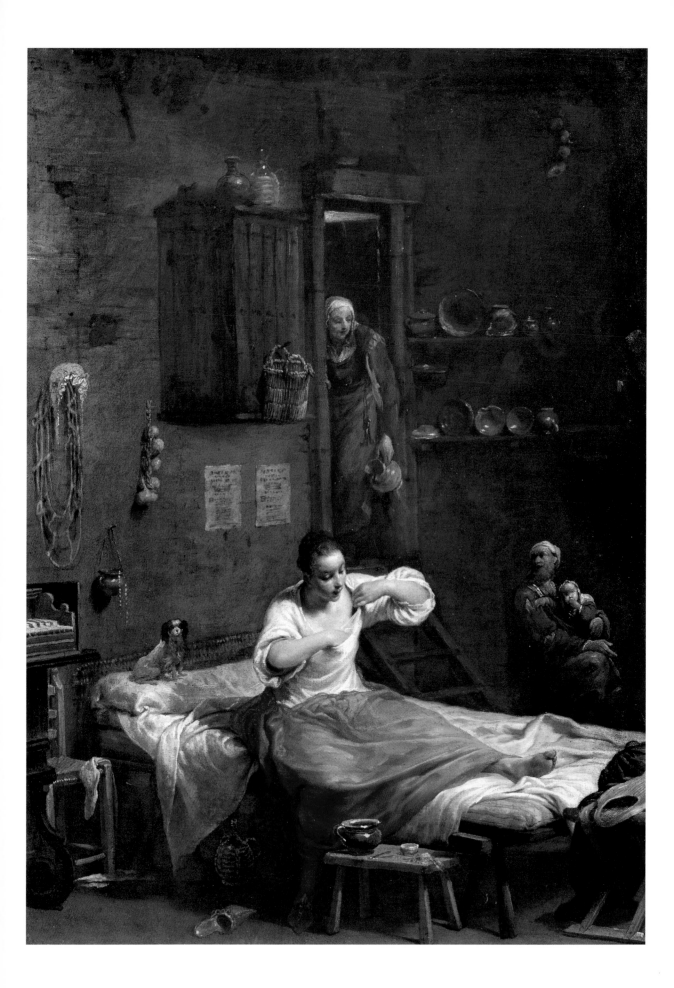

The seventeenth and eighteenth centuries in Italy

The taste for Italian painting had been established by Louis XIV, and was continued throughout the eighteenth century.

However, some 'modern' Italian paintings had already entered the royal collection under Louis XIII – such as the *Public Felicity* **painted for Marie de Médicis by Orazio Gentileschi during his stay in France in 1624-25.** It is also known that Guido Reni, and later Guercino, had been invited, but in vain, to come and work in France.

The taste for the Roman and Bolognese 'Grand Manner', which continued to inspire artists in France until the end of the eighteenth century, had spread amongst Parisian collectors by the mid-1600s. The Roman painter Giovanni Francesco Romanelli, having painted the ceiling of a gallery (now the Bibliothèque Nationale) for Cardinal Mazarin, was employed to decorate, in fresco, the Appartements d'Eté of Queen Anne of Austria in the Louvre. Another dazzling example of this predilection of contemporary French collectors was the gallery built in about 1643/45 by Louis-Philippeaux de La Vrillère, and decorated with a series of vast canvases illustrating episodes of Roman history. He commissioned the most famous painters working in Rome and Bologna at the time–Guercino, Pietro da Cortona, Alessandro Turchi, and Carlo Maratta–to complete the series begun by Guido Reni's *The abduction of Helen* and Poussin's *The school-master of Falerii*. This series of ten great compositions was taken to the Louvre during the Revolution but has, unfortunately, since been dispersed. The Louvre has kept the paintings by Poussin, Reni, and Turchi, and one each by Guercino and Pietro da Cortona, but the others have been sent to various provincial museums and are replaced by copies.

The wholesale dispersal of the Mazarin and Jabach collections introduced several major seventeenth-century paintings to Louis XIV's collection, including the *Death of the Virgin* by Caravaggio and the four paintings from the *Story of Hercules* by Guido Reni, which had come from Charles I's collection and previously from the Dukes of Mantua. Later, many paintings by the best-loved Bolognese artists–Carracci, Reni, Guercino, Domenichino, and Francesco Albani–were to adorn Louis XIV's collection, bought from, or given by, various French and Italian connoisseurs. Thus, in 1665, Prince Pamphili sent him from Rome *Hunting* and *Fishing* by Annibale Carracci, as well as Caravaggio's *The fortune teller;* and André Le Nôtre, the King's gardener, left him his paintings by Albani in 1693. Amongst the works of other Italian schools in Louis XIV's collection were important paintings by Fetti, such as his *Melancholy,* Rosa, Lanfranco, Baciccia, and Castiglione.

<
Giuseppe Maria Crespi
Bologna, 1665–
Bologna, 1747
The flea
circa 1720/5

Canvas
54 x 40 cm
Presented by the Société des Amis du Louvre, 1970

Under Louis XV, the purchases from the estate of the Prince de Carignan in 1741 introduced other paintings by Pietro da Cortona, Maratta, and above all, Castiglione, one of the chief sources of inspiration for the French in the eighteenth century, including his *The expulsion of the merchants from the temple* and the *Adoration*. Systematic purchases made by d'Angiviller under Louis XVI, with a view to making the future Museum more comprehensive, also included Seicento paintings such as *The Raising of Lazarus* by Guercino and works of the beginning of the eighteenth century such as *The expulsion of Heliodorus* by Solimena.

One masterpiece which fortuitously entered the collections of the Museum during the Revolution was the brilliant series of *Venetian festivals* by Francesco Guardi, illustrating the ceremonies of the Coronation of the Doge Alvise Mocenigo in 1763. This cycle has now been dispersed, as several of the twelve canvases were sent to provincial museums during the Empire. However, a programme of exchanges, already begun, could ensure the reconstitution of the whole cycle.

The great Bolognese painters of the seventeenth century constituted one of the short-lived glories of the Musée Napoléon. Most of the paintings taken in Italy were returned in 1815, but some important canvases by Ludovico and Annibale Carracci, *The Virgin appears to St Hyacinth* and *The Virgin appears to St Luke and St Catherine,* and by Guercino, *The Patron saints of Modena,* remain in Paris and make the Emilian collection in the Louvre the most complete outside Bologna itself.

It is characteristic of the French preference for the Bolognese painters that, with a few exceptions such as Salvatore Rosa, the other schools of the Seicento were excluded. The representation of this period, so lacking in Lombard, Neapolitan and Florentine paintings, is still marked by this imbalance. Efforts have been made to redress the balance, lealding to the acquisition of important works by Serodine, Manfredi, Biliverti, Giulio-Cesare Procaccini and Cavalino.

During the course of the last century, little was added to the collection of seventeenth-century Italian paintings, though the same period saw the consolidation of the eighteenth-century section. The reign of Louis-Philippe saw the acquisition of Marieschi's *View of Santa Maria Salute* (then attributed to Canaletto) and important works by Pannini. *The Last Supper* by Giambattista Tiepolo entered the collection in 1877 and later the sketch for a ceiling, *The triumph of religion.* Only in the last fifty years has the collection of the Settecento finally achieved some measure of consistency. New works by the two Tiepolos, Pellegrini, Sebastiano Ricci and Pittoni have completed the Venetian collection, now dominated by Piazzetta's monumental *Assumption of the Virgin* (returned by the musée de Lille in an exchange). Pietro Longhi's *The Presentation* and works by Canaletto from the Péreire and Lyon donations have finally taken their place in the collection. Worthy also of note are the excellent paintings given in usufruct by the Schlageter and Kaufmann collection in 1984, including works by Tiepolo, Pittoni, Pellegrini, Solimena, Creti and Giaquinto. The Neapolitan school, too, is better represented, by Mura and Mondo, as are the realists – so long eclipsed by the glory of Venice – such as Magnasco's eerie *Bohemian meal,* the theatrical naturalism of Traversi's *The sitting* and the portraiture of Ghislandi. A place has also been made for the *Portrait of Charles Crowle* by Pompeo Batoni, the central figure in Roman Painting.

∧
Michelangelo Merisi,
called **Caravaggio**
Caravaggio, 1570 or 1571 –
Porto Ercole, 1610
The fortune teller
Circa 1594/5

Canvas
99 x 131 cm
Collection of Louis XIV
Purchased in 1665

<
Michelangelo Merisi,
called **Caravaggio**
Caravaggio, 1570 or 1571 –
Porto Ercole, 1610
The Death of the Virgin
1605/6

Canvas
369 x 245 cm
Collection of Louis XIV
Purchased in 1671

>

Orazio Gentileschi
Pisa, 1563 – London, 1639
*Public Felicity triumphant
over dangers*
Circa 1624/5

Canvas
268 x 170 cm
Collection of Marie de Médicis

v

Orazio Gentileschi
Pisa, 1563 – London, 1639
Rest on the Flight
Circa 1628

Canvas
158 x 225 cm
*Collection of Louis XIV
Purchased in 1671*

>
Bartolomeo Manfredi
Ostiano, 1582 –
Rome, after 1622
David triumphant
Circa 1615

Canvas
128 x 97 cm
Purchased in 1990

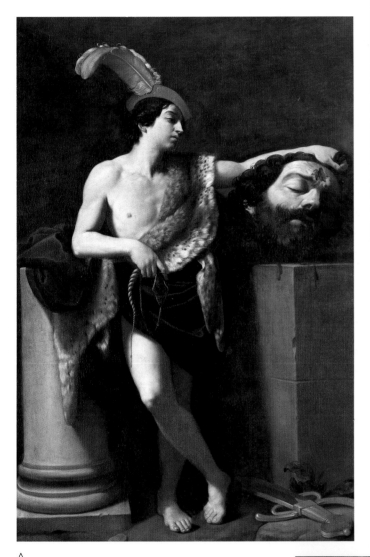

∧
Guido Reni
Bologna, 1575 – Bologna, 1642
*David holding the head
of Goliath*
Circa 1601/5

Canvas
237 x 137 cm
Collection of Louis XIV

>
Giovanni Serodine
Ascona, 1600 – Rome, 1630
Jesus among the doctors
Circa 1625

Canvas
145 x 224 cm
Purchased in 1983

∧
Giulio Cesare Pocaccini
Bologna, circa 1570 –
Milan, 1625
The Annunciation
Circa 1620 (?)

Canvas
23 x 16 cm
*Presented by the Société
des Amis du Louvre*

The Italian Secento is magnificently represented in the Louvre, but coverage is unbalanced: while Bologna and Rome are very fully represented, other schools like Naples, Florence and Venice are only patchily so. This sparkling and elegant Annunciation, *the gift of the Amis du Louvre, is a major work of one of the greatest painters of the Lombard school, hitherto barely represented.*

∧

Annibale Carracci
Bologna, 1560 – Rome, 1609
Fishing
Circa 1585/8

Canvas
135 x 253 cm
Collection of Louis XIV
Purchased in 1665

∧

Annibale Carracci
Bologna, 1560 – Rome, 1609
The hunt
Circa 1585

Canvas
136 x 253 cm
Collection of Louis XIV
Acquired in 1665

^

Domenico Zampieri,
called **Domenichino**
Bologna, 1581 – Rome, 1641
Landscape with Erminia
and the shepherds
Circa 1620

Canvas
123 x 181 cm
Collection of Louis XIV
Purchased in 1661

>

Ludovico Carracci
Bologna, 1555 – Bologna, 1619
The Virgin appears
to St Hyacinth
1594

Canvas
375 x 223 cm
From San Domenico, Bologna
Entered in 1797

∧
Annibale Carrracci
Bologna, 1560 – Rome, 1609
*The Virgin appears to St Luke
and St Catherine*
1592

Canvas
401 x 226 cm
*From the Cathedral of Reggio Emilia
Entered in 1797*

<
Gian-Francesco Barbieri,
called **Guercino**
Cento, 1591 – Bologna, 1666
The patron saints
of the town of Modena
Circa 1651/2

Canvas
332 x 230 cm
From the Ducal Gallery, Modena
Entered in 1797

>
Guido Reni
Bologna, 1575 – Bologna, 1642
The abduction of Helen
1631

Canvas
253 x 265 cm
Seized during the French Revolution
(collection of the Duc de Penthièvre)

<
Gian-Francesco Barbieri,
called **Guercino**
Cento, 1591 –
Bologna, 1666
The Raising of Lazarus
Circa 1619

Canvas
199 x 233 cm
Collection of Louis XVI
Purchased in 1785

>
Guido Reni
Bologna, 1575 – Bologna, 1642
Detanetra and the centaur Nessus
1621

Canvas
259 x 193 cm
Collection of Louis XIV
Purchased in 1662

∧
**Giovanni Francesco
Romanelli**
Rome, circa 1610 –
Rome, 1662
Diana and Actaeon
Circa 1655

Mural painting
450 x 355 cm
*Section of the ceiling of
the Petite Galerie in the Louvre*

<
**Pietro Berettino
da Cortona**
Cortona, 1596 – Rome, 1669
*Romulus and Remus given
shelter by Faustulus*
Circa 1643

Canvas
251 x 266 cm
*Seized during the French
Revolution (collection
of the Duc de Penthièvre)*

>
Giovanni-Battista Gaulli,
called **Baciccia**
Genoa, 1639 – Rome, 1709
*The preaching of St John
the Baptist*
Circa 1690

Canvas
181 x 172 cm
*Collection of Louis XIV
Entered before 1695*

^
**Giovanni Benedetto
Castiglione**
Genoa, circa 1611 (?) –
Mantua, 1663 or 1665
*The Adoration
of the Shepherds*
Circa 1645/50

Copper
68 x 52 cm
*Collection of Louis XV
Purchased in 1742*

>
Domenico Fetti
Rome, circa 1589 –
Venice, 1623
Melancholy
Circa 1620

Canvas
168 x 128 cm
*Collection of Louis XIV
Purchased in 1685*

<

Francesco Solimena
Pagani, 1657 – Naples, 1747
The expulsion of Heliodorus
Circa 1723/5

Canvas
150 x 200 cm
Collection of Louis XVI
Purchased in 1786

>

Allessandro Magnasco
Genoa, 1667 –
Genoa, 1749
A toast to the betrothed
couple, known as
'Le repas des bohémiens'
Circa 1730/40

Canvas
86 x 118 cm
Presented by M et Mme
Christian Lazard, 1927

<

Salvator Rosa
Naples, 1615 – Rome, 1673
The shade of Samuel
appears to Saul
1668

Canvas
275 x 191 cm
Collection of Louis XIV
Purchased before 1683

>

Gaspare Traversi
Naples, circa 1722/24 –
Rome, 1770
The sitting
1754

Canvas
99 x 130 cm
Presented by the Société
des Amis du Louvre, 1990

This painting was commissioned from Piazzetta by the Prince Elector of Cologne to decorate the High Altar of the Church of the Teutonic Order at Sachsenhausen. It is a dazzling example of the great vertical compositions invented by the Romans and Venetians and based on a rhythmic ascending movement which was later adopted by German Baroque architects. In his carlier works Piazzetta had tended to use darker colours, but here lightens his palette while retaining the sold power of the forms.

<
Giambattista Piazzetta
Venice, 1683 – Venice, 1754
*The Assumption
of the Virgin*
1735

Canvas
517 x 245 cm
*From the church of the Germanic
order of Sachsenhausen,
near Frankfurt
Entered in 1796*

>
Giovanni Battista Tiepolo
Venice, 1696 – Madrid, 1770
The Last Supper
Circa 1745/50

Canvas
79 x 88 cm
Purchased in 1877

^
Pietro Longhi
Venice, 1702 – Venice, 1785
The Presentation
Circa 1740

Canvas
64 x 53 cm
Bestowed by the
Office des Biens Privés, 1950

>
Giandomenico Tiepolo
Venice, 1727 – Venice, 1804
Carnival scene
Circa 1745/50

Canvas
805 x 1105 cm
Bequeathed by Alexandre-Robert
Le Roux de Villers, 1938

<
Francesco Guardi
Venice, 1712 – Venice, 1792
*Audience granted by the
Doge to the ambassadors
in the Sala del Collego
of the Doges' Palace*
Circa 1766/70

Canvas
66 x 100 cm
*Seized during the French
Revolution (collection
of Pestre de Seneffe)*

v
Giovanni Paolo Panini
Piacenze, 1691 – Rome, 1764
*A musical fête given
by the Cardinal de la
Rochefoucauld at the
Theatre Argentina,
Rome, on 15 July 1747
in honour of the marriage
of the Dauphin of France*
1747

Canvas
204 x 247 cm
Collection of Louis-Philippe

∧
Francesco Guardi
Venice, 1712 – Venice, 1792
*The Doge on the Bucentaur
at San Niccolò del Lido*
Circa 1766/70

Canvas
67 x 100 cm
*Seized during the French Revolution
(collection of Pestre de Seneffe)*

>
Pompeo Batoni
Lucca, 1708 – Rome, 1787
Portrait of Charles Crowle
1761-2

Canvas
248 x 172 cm
*Presented by the Société
des Amis du Louvre, 1981*

*This painting belongs to a series of twelve canvases,
almost all in the Louvre, which recount the various
episodes in the election of Doge Alvise Mocenigo of
Venice in 1763. In reporting this event Guardi was
inspired by engravings after that other master of
the Venetian view,* veduta, *Antonio Canaletto. An
observant and picturesque record of the traditional
Venetian festival, which was part official ceremony
and part popular rejoicing, this series attests to
the pictorial verve of Guardi and to his sensitivity
to the most fleeting atmospheric effects, worthy of
the Impressionists over a century later.*

The Germanic and Scandinavian countries

The Louvre could not claim, any more than any other museum outside Germany, to illustrate fully the long history of painting in the Germanic countries.

At least the collection of the Louvre has some strong points, however uneven it remains in its overall coverage. These are perhaps best outlined chronologically rather than in order of their entry to the collections as elsewhere. Firstly, a small group of paintings in the International Gothic style are of merit. Curiously, several of these small pictures once passed as French, at a time between the World Wars when enthusiasm for the rediscovered French primitives caused their output to 'increase' at the expense of German and Spanish painters. The panel of *The Virgin with a rose garland with Otto von Hohenstein, Bishop of Merseburg* of circa 1400 is now attributed to a Saxon artist, and that of *The Virgin at her writing-desk* of circa 1420 to an Austrian artist. The small polyptych called the *Chapelle Cardon,* bequeathed by the Belgian collector, Cardon, 1921 is attributed to an artist of the Lower Rhine. A *Virgin and Child* belonging to the most refined courtly Gothic style of central Europe came from Bohemia in the second quarter of the fifteenth century.

The important collection of the early masters working in Cologne begins with a minute *Miracle of St Voult,* which was also once attributed to a French artist but was in fact painted in about 1440 by a follower of Stefan Lochner. This collection represents the work of most of the anonymous masters of the end of the fifteenth century who lived in the rich Cologne centre of painting. They include the Master of St Bartholomew, whose monumental *Descent from the Cross* was in Paris from the sixteenth century; the Master of the Holy Family, whose *Altarpiece of the Seven Joys of Mary* was purchased in 1912; the Master of the Legend of St Bruno; the Master of St Severinus, whose *The Presentation in the Temple* was a gift of the Société des Amis du Louvre in 1972; and the Master of St Ursula, whose two *Scenes from the life of St Ursula* were part of a cycle dispersed among several museums. Although born in Cologne, the Master of St Ursula also seems to have painted the *Pietà,* which was undertaken around 1500 in Paris for the church of Saint-Germain-des-Prés and which has a delicate view of Paris in the background. Finally, the last painter of the Cologne School during the Renaissance, Barthel Bruyn, is represented by the double Portrait of the large Gail family, purchased in 1916.

The other fifteenth-century German schools are hardly represented at all; a visit to the museum of Dijon will find a varied collection of German primitives in France. Among several panels which are in the collection, the following are outstanding:

the *Annunciation with two Saints* by the Ulm master, Barthel Weitblom, given by the Marchesa Arconati-Visconti in 1916, and a *St George rescuing the Princess* by a master of the Upper Rhine at the end of the fifteenth century. A mysterious *Portrait of a woman,* bought in 1920 and called *The Delphic Sibyl,* would seem to be a fifteenth-century painting reflecting the influence of the Master of Flémalle although it was earlier attributed to Ludger Tom Ring, a painter working in Munster in the mid-sixteenth century.

Dürer and Holbem dominate the collection of great Renaissance masters. The *Self portrait* of 1493 by Dürer, purchased by the Louvre in 1922, is undoubtedly the first independent self-portrait painted north of the Alps (excluding that of Fouquet, painted on enamel and also in the Louvre). The Cabinet des Dessins already had two canvases by the artist: the masterly *Portrait of an old man,* dated 1520, and the curiously bearded *Head of a youth* of 1527.

The five Holbein portraits are amongst the glories of the Museum and entered the royal collection in the seventeenth century. The *portrait of Erasmus* was a gift from Charles I to his brother-in-law Louis XIII in exchange for Leonardo's *John the Baptist* (which later returned to Louis XIV). The other paintings – *William Warham, Henry Wyatt, Nicolas Kratzer,* and *Anne of Cleves* – had belonged to the Earl of Arundel, a passionate collector and inspiration and rival of Charles I, and were bought for the collection of Louis XIV at the Jabach sale. From the Mazarin collection Louis XIV acquired another masterpiece of the German Renaissance, a table painted for Cardinal Albert of Brandenburg by Hans Sebald Beham with minute and fanciful *Scenes from the life of David.*

The collection also contains a group of paintings by Lucas Cranach which include a *Venus* purchased in 1806 and a *Portrait of a young girl* bought in 1910. The other works of the first half of the sixteenth century from a more disparate group, from the *Adoration of the Magi* by Ulrich Apt of Augsburg, purchased in 1807, to the allegory of *The knight, the young girl, and Death* by Hans Baldung Grien. The recent purchase of Wolf Huber's *Lamentation* brings to mind the lyricism and visual liberties of the masters of the Danube School, now fashionable once again.

The seventeenth century in Germany, whose diversity has been revealed in various recent exhibitions, is represented only by some powerful still lifes by George Flegel and Gottfried von Wedig. Particularly note-worthy among the eighteenth-century German and Austrian paintings are a sketch of the *Annunciation* by Marlbertsch, purchased in 1987, and a series of portraits which deserves to be better known. They range from psychological studies in the works of Balthasar Denner and Christian Seybold and official effigies by Mengs, to the international type of the elegant *fin-de-siècle* portrait in the works of Angelica Kauffmann and Anton Graff whose formula is re-echoed in the work of Johann Baptist Lampi and the Russian artists Leviski and Borovikovski.

Nineteenth-century painting in the Germanic countries figures in the national collection only in the works of the second half of the century by Mackart, Böcklin, and Liebermann, which are now on view in the Musée d'Orsay. The greatest German painter of the beginning of the century, and one of the geniuses of European Romanticism, Caspar David Friedrich, is still an isolated figure in the collection: the *Tree of crows* was purchased from the Louvre in 1975.

Moreover, the admirable 'Golden Age' of Danish painting has begun to find its expression in several small works by Kobke, Jensen and Eckersberg, notably the latter's *Seated nude model,* an intimate and highly personal vision of David's neo-classicism.

∧

**Master of the
Holy Family**
Active in Cologne between
1475 and circa 1510
*Altarpiece of the
Seven Joys of Mary*
Circa 1480

Wood
127 x 182 cm
Purchased in 1912

<

**Master of
St Bartholomew**
Active in Cologne between
1475 and 1510
*The Descent
from the Cross*
Circa 1500/05

Wood
227 x 210 cm
*From the church of
the Val de Grâce, Paris*

Lucas Cranach
Kronach, 1472 – Weimar, 1553
*Portrait presumed to be
of Magdalena Luther,
daughter of Martin Luther*
Circa 1540 (?)

Wood
39 x 25 cm
Purchased in 1910

<
Lucas Cranach
Kronach, 1472 –
Weimar, 1553
Venus
1529

Wood
33 x 26 cm
Entered in 1806

>
German School
15th century (?)
Portrait of a woman,
called *The Delphic Sibyl*

Wood
44 x 31 cm
*Attributed to
Ludger Tom Ring
the Elder
Purchased in 1920*

∧
**Hans Baldung
Grien**
Gmünd, 1484/5 –
Strasbourg, 1545
*The knight,
the young girl,
and Death*
Circa 1505

Wood
355 x 296 cm
Purchased in 1924

<
**Wolf Huber
Feldkirch (?)**
Circa 1485 –
Passau, 1553
*The Lamentation
of Christ*
1524

Wood
105 x 86 cm
Purchased in 1968

^
Hans Holbein
Augsburg, 1497 –
London, 1543
Nicholas Kratzer
1528

Wood
83 x 67 cm
Collection of Louis XIV
Purchased in 1671

>
Hans Holbein
Augsburg, 1497 –
London, 1543
Erasmus
1523

Wood
42 x 32 cm
Collection of Louis XIV
Purchased in 1671

Λ
Hans Sebald Beham
Nuremberg, 1500 –
Frankfurt, 1550
*Scenes from the life
of David*
1534

Painted table, wood
128 x 131 cm
Collection of Louis XIV

∧
Georg Flegel
Olmütz, 1566 –
Frankfurt am Main, 1638
Still life with fish
1637

Wood
19 x 15 cm
Purchased in 1981

>
**Christoffer-Wilhelm
Eckersberg**
Sundeved, 1783 –
Copenhagen, 1853
Seated nude model
1839

Canvas
45 x 33 cm
Purchased in 1987

^

Caspar David Friedrich
Greifswald, 1774 –
Dresden, 1840
The tree of crows
Circa 1822

Canvas
59 x 74 cm
Purchased in 1975

Great Britain

British painting is very unevenly represented in most of the great museums outside the English-speaking countries, and is often considered to be the poor relation in European art. The Louvre, with an extensive collection, is an exception to this rule.

While the Louvre does not offer a sufficiently varied or detailed illustration of the various trends of the British school it is, to a certain extent, the exception to this rule, as its collection is quite extensive. It begins with a good William Scrots, the *Portrait of Edward VI,* and continues until the end of the nineteenth century (the paintings from the second half of the century, from the Pre-Raphaelites onwards, are now on show at the Musée d'Orsay). It is true that figures of the eminence of Hogarth and Richard Wilson or of William Blake and Samuel Palmer are still absent, but a fair number of other very important painters, from Allan Ramsay to Turner, are represented by works which are of artistic value even if they are not always exceptional or sufficiently numerous.

With the exception of the purchase of a small painting by Bonington, *François I and the Duchesse d'Etampes* in 1849, and that of his *Parterre d'eau at Versailles* in 1872, as well as two paintings by Constable, the collection was built up in two distinct stages: during the years 1880-1910 and since the second World War.

The first stage corresponded to a great vogue for English painting – or at least a certain view of English painting – which was upheld in Paris by journals such as *L'Art* (later *Les Arts*) and important dealers such as Charles Sedelmeyer. The organisation of an exhibition at Bagatelle (1905) and, above all, the large number of English paintings which entered the great Parisian collections of the time, bore witness to this fashion. One of these, the collection created with such enthusiasm by Camille Groult, was to become as famous for its Gainsboroughs and Turners as for its Watteaus. It was in the fervently pro-British climate that the Louvre purchased, in Paris or London, some of its most remarkable portraits, for example *Mr and Mrs Angerstein* by Laurence in 1896. *Sir John Stanley* by Ramsay in 1897, and *Captain Robert May* by Raeburn in 1908. At the same time the Museum received a number of canvases which, we can now admit, say more for the generosity of their anglophile donors than for the merits of their presumed artists. Happily, certain paintings of the highest quality were also given at this time: the famous *Master Hare* by Reynolds in the Baron Alphonse de Rothschild Bequest of 1905, and several works by Bonington. Soon after the Second World War the Louvre acquired a number of pictures which recall the taste of the great French collectors at the end of the last century for the elegance and pictorial verve of the best English portraitists of the eighteenth century: the sumptuous *Portrait of Lady Alston* by Gainsborough, a masterpiece of the Bath period given in 1947 by the heirs of Baron Robert de Rothschild; his delightful *Conversation in a park,* a rare early work which may be a self-portrait of the artist and his wife; and the *Portrait of Charles William Bell* by Lawrence.

In the last thirty years or so the keepers of the Department of Paintings have tried to complete this heritage more systematically. On the one hand, they have strengthened the representation of certain artists, like Constable (who was so important at the birth of French romanticism for the visual liberation of the artist confronted by nature), with his *View in the park at Helmingham* bought in 1948 and *View of Salisbury* from the Percy Moore Turner bequest of 1952, and Lawrence, with his presumed *Portrait of the Angerstein children*, purchased by the Société des Amis du Louvre. On the other hand they have attempted to fill the most lamentable gaps. The absence of Turner, perhaps the greatest of English artists, had long been regretted as he was linked to France by his admiration for Claude Lorrain. He is now represented in the Louvre by one of his late works in which, typically, the dissolution of form gives the appearance of an unfinished painting.

The history of English painting in the eighteenth century has changed considerably in the last thirty years, inasmuch as the scale of values which determined it has altered. Artists like Stubbs and Joseph Wright of Derby who had been neglected for a long time have now regained their rightful place in the hierarchy of excellence, relegating fashionable portraits, whose technique was weak and appeal superficial, to the background. We have also rediscovered the sharp simplicity of Zoffany's conversation pieces and, at the opposite extreme, the heated visions of the anglicised Swiss, Fuseli. The recent purchases of *A view of the Lake of Nemi* and a *Portrait of a man* by Wright, the *Portrait of the Reverend Randall Burroughes with his son* by Zoffany and Fuseli's *Lady Macbeth,* together with the gift by the Duchess of Windsor of the *Portrait of Viscount Curzon with his mare Marta* by Stubbs, mark the beginning of a programme of acquisitions which aims to diversify the Louvre's representation of the complex and rich period of the end of the eighteenth century.

Similarly, an opening has been made into nineteenth-century painting in the United States with the purchase in 1975 of the romantic *Cross in solitude* painted in 1848 by Thomas Cole. The American artists of the turn of the century, Thomas Eakins, Winslow Homer and Whistler, are now on view in the Musée d'Orsay.

∧
Thomas Gainsborough
Sudbury, 1727 –
London, 1788
Lady Alston
Circa 1760/5

Canvas
226 x 168 cm
Presented by the heirs of
Baron Robert de Rothschild

This work dates from Gainsborough's mature period, when he resided in Bath as a fashionable portraitist of the aristocracy. Following the elegant van Dyck tradition, he places the model in a broad landscape background. However, the strong contrasts of the lighting of the figure and the flashing effect achieved on the silk of her dress against the deep, impenetrable forest behind her, make this mysterious and poetic portrait a totally original work.

<
Joshua Reynolds
Plympton, 1723 –
London, 1792
Master Hare
Circa 1788/9

Canvas
77 x 63 cm
*Bequeathed by
Baron Alphonse de Rothschild,
1905*

∨
Joseph Wright,
called **Wright of Derby**
Derby, 1734 – Derby, 1797
View of the Lake of Nemi
Circa 1790/5

Canvas
105 x 128 cm
Purchased in 1970

∧
Johann Heinrich Fuseli
Zurich, 1741 – London, 1825
Lady Macbeth
1784

Canvas
221 x 160 cm
Purchased in 1970

> Thomas Lawrence
Bristol, 1768 –
London, 1830
*Portrait of the children
of John Angerstein*
1808

Canvas
194 x 144 cm
*Presented by the Société
des Amis du Louvre, 1975*

< Thomas Lawrence
Bristol, 1769 –
London, 1830
*Mr and Mrs John Julius
Angerstein*
1792

Canvas
252 x 160 cm
Purchased in 1896

The Portrait of Mr & Mrs John Julius Angerstein *is one of Lawrence's masterpieces and depicts, together with his wife, one of the founders of Lloyds insurance market. He was a great collector and the purchase in 1828 of his collection formed the nucleus of paintings for the National Gallery in London. The* Angerstein children, *presented in 1975 by the Société des Amis du Louvre, are the young children of this couple.*

∧
Henry Raeburn
Stockbridge, 1756 –
Edinburgh, 1823
Young girl holding flowers
Circa 1798/1800 (?)

Canvas
92 x 71 cm
*Bequeathed by Mme Pierre
Lebaudy, 1962*

∨
John Constable
East Bergholt, 1776 –
London, 1837
View of Salisbury
Circa 1820 (?)

Canvas
35 x 51 cm
*Bequeathed by Percy
Moore Turner, 1952*

<
Richard Parkes Bonington
Arnold, 1802 –
London, 1828
On the Adriatic
Circa 1826

Card
30 x 43 cm
Purchased in 1926

∨
Joseph Mallord William Turner
London, 1775 –
London, 1851
Landscape with a river and a bay in the background
Circa 1835/40

Canvas
93 x 123 cm
Purchased in 1967

Index of Artists

References in roman
are to pages where
the artists are cited,
italic references
are to illustrations.

Colour separation : Daiichi Process, Singapour
Printed by Editoriale Lloyd, Italy
December 2000
Dépôt légal: March 2000